Wait for What?

WAIT FOR WHAT?

PATRICIA A. DALEY
Xulon Press

Xulon Press
2301 Lucien Way #415
Maitland, FL 32751
407.339.4217
www.xulonpress.com

© 2017 by Patricia A Daley

All rights reserved solely by the author. The author guarantees all contents are original and do not infringe upon the legal rights of any other person or work. No part of this book may be reproduced in any form without the permission of the author. The views expressed in this book are not necessarily those of the publisher.

Scripture quotations taken from the New King James Version (NKJV). Copyright © 1982 by Thomas Nelson, Inc. Used by permission. All rights reserved.

Edited by Xulon Press.

Printed in the United States of America.

ISBN-13: 9781545612071

Dedication

This book is dedicated to you,
my many friends, in my homeland Jamaica,
in my new land the USA, and indeed to
all my friends everywhere.

CONTENTS

Author's Note ix
Preface xiii
Acknowledgments xvii
Introduction xxi
Chapter 1: Who Likes to Wait? 1
Chapter 2: He Captivates Her Heart . . . 14
Chapter 3: Carissa Starts to Like Boys 36
Chapter 4: Has God Forgotten? 50
Chapter 5: Life's Twists and Turns 64
Chapter 6: Life's Uncertainties 81
Chapter 7: Is This Wait Too Long? 97
Chapter 8: The Anxiety of Waiting 115
Chapter 9: When "No" Brings Joy 134
Chapter 10: Wait for What? 152
Discussion Questions for Small
    Group Study 171

Author Note

This book was written for a broad group of people including: those who are single, those already married, those not yet married but wanting to be married, those not married and not wanting to be married, and some who are already married and want to get out. Sounds crazy, you say. Maybe you are right. But then again, maybe not, so read on.

I believe that if you read this book to the very end, you will benefit in some way, for this book was written with you foremost in mind. I believe you will personally identify with some of the people I have written about to such an extent that the knowledge you gain through your faithful reading will enrich your life. My conviction is that the life issues exposed in this book are challenges you are either facing now or will be facing shortly in your life.

So, secure a copy of this book for yourself, and then find a convenient, comfortable place in your house where you can sit back or lie down. Perhaps grab a pillow, and then read yourself into a new vision of gripping, informative, and profitable realities.

If you live in New York or some other major city, you might want to read this book on a long train ride to work or when you go to visit a friend in another borough. Of course, if you are fortunate enough to have long hours to spare, as when you are on vacation, go ahead and read your eyes out, allowing the contents of this book to reach your mind and heart.

Wherever you might be, understand that this book is intended to stir your emotions. It may cause tears to fall from your eyes, or it may spark new thoughts in your mind, generating ideas that inspire you to do some personal research. At times, it might even cause you to choke with laughter. Furthermore, it may constrain you to discuss what you're learning with family members, close friends, colleagues, or sincere acquaintances.

To sum up, this book is written to inform and inspire you humanly, culturally, psychologically, and personally. I pray it will be deeply profitable to you in all areas of your life.

Preface

"You have to kiss a lot of frogs to find a prince" is a statement often made to comfort many Christian young women after they have gone through a series of breakups. However, going through a series of unsuccessful relationships is not something to be proud of, especially when you feel that you can never get the "dating thing" right and the same type of man keeps knocking at your door.

You know the type. He dresses the part, smells like ginger and rosemary, has perfect teeth, and treats you like a queen. Mr. Fabulous (in your head) meets Mommy and Daddy and even takes your little brother to soccer practice. He sits beside you in church and grunts amen under his breath. He sings in the choir and spends time praying about your possible blissful future together.

Then, the unpredictable happens. His heart is split in two. Half of him wants to be married, and the other part wants to continue to look around for Mrs. Wonderful. You, obviously, are not the one. You begin the process of waiting for a mate all over again.

We spend most of our lives waiting. A woman may wait for years to find a partner. Then she has to wait for a baby, and sometimes she has to wait until her husband decides which house they will buy. She has to wait until her children grow up and go away to college to afford some free time for herself. With the passage of time, she realizes she has forgotten to live.

Singles, in particular, seem to spend a lot of time waiting, confused by the events going on around them. For example, a friend's husband dies, and in the span of a year or two, she remarries. In the meantime, the single woman has never even been married once. *What is wrong with me?* is often the cry of many singles. *Why do I have to wait so long? Has God forgotten me?* These are the cries and the questions that roll in their hearts, while God seems silent.

The purpose of this book is to minister to women who have had to wait for various things in their lives. What is the Lord saying to us as we wait? What lessons does He want us to learn? What purpose does He have in mind for us as we wait?

Though the storyline focuses on a single Christian woman named Carissa, who is waiting for a mate, my intention is to encourage all women of faith, as well as those interested in Christianity, to experience the power of God. The story contained in these pages is part biography and part fiction, but I have changed the names of many individuals for reasons of privacy.

Acknowledgements

To my editor: Thank you for taking a personal interest in the contents of this story. Your personal touch and style brought a new perspective as I articulated what I really want to say to the readers. Furthermore, your honesty gave me a sense of purpose as I crafted the lines of this story to make it into a unique bestseller.

To Mr. Billy Hall, my spiritual father, who took a special interest in this story: Your enthusiasm and shared vision were the driving force in the completion of this book. Thanks for your prayers and support, as well as your fatherly advice as I sought to share this profound message with women of all caliber and race. Thank you especially for putting that motivational book in my hands as I sought to find my way as a teenager. That was the book that propelled me to pursue my life dreams without hesitation and to take my leap of faith those many years. Thank you!

To my second mother Mrs. Asenath Scott, who has been my inspiration for the most part of my teenage and adult life: Without your continued support in my different life journey, I would not have had this vision and courage to pursue a career in writing.

To my biological mother, Ms. Claudette Malcolm, who took the time to listen to me read, chapter after chapter and make the necessary corrections that were needed: Thanks for being my cheerleader as I penned the pages of this story and thanks for your prayers.

To Claudette Jolly, who is one of my most encouraging friends: Thank you for taking the time to listen, critique, and give practical suggestions as I reorganized and shifted parts of the story line to create flow. Thank you, my dearest friend, for the laughter, and the tears, as you listened night after night to the chapters. This was very encouraging.

To my spiritual fathers, Bros, Victor Bonett and Donahue Collash, who encouraged and prayed for me as I struggled with many challenging life issues throughout in my Christian walk: Thank you for lending me your ears and for being honest when I needed to act. Thank you for opening your homes to me when I just needed a father to talk to. Your wives were equally welcoming and supportive, and I appreciate that tremendously.

Introduction

Carissa Peyton's story is an inspirational testimony about standing firmly on God's principles throughout the struggles involved in being a single Christian woman. Her journey to find love and family takes her through many detours before she finds fulfillment and self-worth through her love and devotion for her Savior, Jesus Christ.

The story unveils Jesus as the Father who takes a special interest in His children, though mother and father may forsake them. In so doing, it provides individual security to those who feel abandoned and rejected in their pursuit of love and acceptance.

Carissa is a meaningful role model for readers as she grapples with the pain of waiting, which later strengthens her relationship with her Lord. Furthermore, as Carissa's story unfolds, the author connects with the experience of Bible characters who, like Carissa, struggled while waiting. Their lives minister to the reader as they reveal how each overcame in his or her trial of waiting on the Lord.

The first chapter documents the various issues a woman may encounter in "waiting" as she struggles to meet the demands of life's expectations. This is followed by another eight chapters, which take us through Carissa's journey as she waits for Mr. Right. The final chapter answers the question of why wait?

A few open-ended questions are included at the end of the story to support small-group discussions of the varied issues women face as they wait for their dreams to be realized.

Chapter 1

Who Likes to Wait?

According to Webster's dictionary, *waiting* means "to stay or rest in expectation; to stop or remain stationary till the arrival of some person or event."

Frankly, I do not like to wait. Nonetheless, I frequently experience having to wait for a considerable amount of time. In New York, where I now live, I have often waited in long lines at bus stops, fast-food restaurants, and ticket windows. Waiting for either an arriving or departing subway train has been another common occurrence.

This waiting, however, is nothing new in my life. In my undergraduate days, I sometimes asked a friend to hold my space in the lunch line so that I could run back to my dorm, grab a quick nap, use the restroom, and get back in time for the meal. Such incidents were all too common for most of us students, so we did not regard it as anything unusual. It was just part of our youthful coping with the detestable waiting process.

Having to wait for long periods of time can register in our minds as embarrassing or uncomfortable. In this twenty-first century of fast-paced, high-speed technology, waiting is torment for many of us. At the tip of a finger, we have access to computers, smartphones, and other technological devices that lull us into thinking everything happens instantly.

Sometimes waiting looks like a vain undertaking. You look around the church, the workplace, and even in your own family and see so many single women who have waited in vain for marriage. An older woman once asked me, "Child, when are you going to get married? Are you going to wait until I am dead before you find Mr. Harmony?" Of course, I was devastated, but I understood that she meant well and did not want me to experience the same fate as those women who seem to have waited in vain.

Then there are those younger women, still in their twenties and early thirties, who start to hit the panic button because they look ahead to the late forties and fifties and see no hope in sight. What should these girls do? Should they run off and get somebody, anybody, because maybe, just perhaps, that man will come to know the Lord when he sees how much she loves Him? Still musing, should that girl give in only to later discover that she has become the daughter-in-law of the prince of this dark world and is faced with misery for the rest of her life?

Waiting is experienced by everyone. The child who waits for a parent to return from a long trip, and never sees or hears them coming, often faces serious anxiety. The wife who waits for her womb to open after years of trying, yet nothing happens, often becomes frustrated. The woman who waits for her son to be released from prison, and is turned down by the parole board, often faces serious pain and suffering.

Waiting can be seen as an enemy or even friend, depending on a person's attitude toward it. It can be termed as torturous or grievous. However, it does not matter how we view it, waiting is inevitable. And, the questions many ask as they wait is penned in this poem, "Wait for What?"

Wait for What?
When Life seems to be passing you by,
while others live on, wait!
Wait for what?

WAIT FOR WHAT?

When desolate days are filled with pain and sighing, wait!
Wait for what?
When friends drift away and a lover never comes by, wait!
Wait for what?
When the phone is as silent as the dead sea, while you stare, wait!
Wait for what?
When the walls of your room are all you can see all night, wait!
Wait for what?
When prayers and sobbing keep you all day on your knees, wait!
Wait for what?
When loneliness rest on you like an unwelcome friend, wait!
Wait for what?
When isolation and desolation never seems to end, wait!
Wait for what?

> When the monotony of each day seems like a refrain, wait!
> Wait for what?

Carissa Peyton was no stranger to waiting. Her experience did not begin with the desire for a mate however, the absence of her parents would cause her to experience a unique type of childhood longing and desire for security.

Carissa grew up in Jamaica West Indies, an island known for the beautiful Blue Mountain Peak, gorgeous sunny weather, crystal clear beaches, sparkling night life, and warm and friendly people. However, like many islanders, people migrate to larger countries for job opportunities and to advance their education. Carissa's parents were part of this great migration to the United States of America. So, Carissa grew up without them.

Her father left long before Carissa saw her first tooth and before she could crawl and creep independently. Her mother Tina stayed for a while, but decided to run for it when Carissa was only nine years old.

One morning while Carissa was on summer vacation, her sleep was disturbed by the pulling and pushing of furniture to make way for a large suitcase that her mother was trying to drag to the door. "Where are you going, Mama?" the girl inquired as she noticed a sheepish look on her mother's face.

"Carissa, I wanted to tell you before, but there is no easy way to break this news to you. In the next two weeks, I have to leave you with your aunt for a little while, but I will come back to get you as soon as I can."

Carissa was petrified. "Mama, you can't leave me!" And the tears began to flow uncontrollably.

"Carissa, I have to go and make a better life for our family, but you and your brother will have to stay with Aunt Baby Lue until I get back. I have no other choice. I will send you toys, books, and pretty dresses and write to you every week. I will make sure to send enough money every month, so that your aunt can take care of you and your brother."

That was the beginning of Carissa's wait. Many weeks turned into months and Aunt Baby Lue did not hear a word from Tina. Every ring tone of the mail man would send Carissa scampering toward the mailbox in search for a letter from her mother.

After three years of supporting the children, Carissa's brother went to live with his father and she went to live with her grandmother. Aunt Baby Lue had four other kids to feed and the financial strain was just too much to bear. She had to abandoned her duties as sole guardian of Tina's children.

Still Carissa waited. Her grandmother was a businesswoman. She owned a large grocery store and invested in various properties. Carissa was the only child at home and was lavished with lots of food and clothing. Her grandmother made sure she was well cared for, but every afternoon, when the mail man passed by, the sound of his bell caused her little heart to skip a million beats. She would often run to the mail box to see if her mother, and by chance her father, wrote her a letter. Her anticipation was short lived time and time again, but Carissa would still wait.

One day, Carissa's grandmother decided to visit her eldest daughter, Layla, in the United States. Carissa was nervous. "What will happen to me if grandma should decide never to return?" She would not sleep and she could not focus at school. Her grandma tried to console her, but Carissa would scream and holler. She did not believe her grandma. The thought of having a second loved one leave for the United States, in promise of return, brought her much grief and she could not be comforted.

Carissa was left to stay with her grandfather for three weeks. She was slightly scared of the man because he would often remind her that her mother abandoned her and she wouldn't amount to much when she grew up. Carissa despised the older man and secretly promised herself that when she grew up, she was going to find an assassin to take care of him.

The first two days were filled with torture for Carissa because she was in a big house with this man alone and there is no telling what he would do to her. The girl lost trust for adults, because she felt that her mother lied to her and now her grandmother went away. She was not sure she was coming back.

Carissa feared for her safety and she feared that her grandmother had abandoned her too, so she slept under the bed with a knife in her hand. She was also afraid to shower because nobody would hear her screams if she was attacked by this man. She would do a quick "hog wash" in the shower as she prepared for school each morning.

Her grandfather sensed what was happening one morning after Carissa left for school. As he was cleaning, he saw a knife under Carissa's pillow. "Maybe, she forgot to put it back in the kitchen when she peeled her orange," he thought. But the next day as he got the bed linens ready to put in the laundry, there was the knife again under Carissa's pillow. "What is wrong with this child?" he reasoned with himself. Later that evening, grandpa called the neighbors to take Carissa until her grandma returned. She was relieved and after two weeks, grandma returned.

"Why did you hide under the bed, Carissa?" her grandma inquired when she heard about the girl's peculiar actions.

"Well, grandma, I do not trust anybody. I have read in the Daily Gleaner that many girls who are abandoned by their parents are abused by uncles, cousins, and even fathers. So, grandma, I am not taking any chances."

Carissa was twelve and was an avid reader. She would read the famous "Dear Pastor" weekly column, and learn about the sexual, physical, and mental abuses that were meted out to young girls who did not have their parents. She became extremely conscious and aware of her surroundings and would dress in larger fitting dresses, just to cover up. This way nobody would desire her.

Her grandma understood and vowed to never leave Carissa in that situation again. After all, it wasn't safe to leave a preteen alone with a man, even though she trusted her husband.

As Carissa grew, her love for reading caused her to succeed in school, but she continued to live with a never- ending heartache as she waited for her mother to call, write, or even send her just a dollar.

After years of waiting for her mother's return, her longing for her parents would shift to another type of passion. She was well into her teenage years, and her new desire for romantic love would take her into a new sphere of waiting.

Join Carissa on her unique journey as she waits for Mr. Right.

CHAPTER 2

He Captivates Her Heart

There comes a time in a little girl's life when she begins to change significantly. It is the moment when the mirror on the wall starts to talk back to her, and she feels like her skirt is too long and her hair is too bland. At the same time, she begins to see the neighbor's son in a different light, and her heart starts to flutter when a boy looks in her direction.

Now at the ripe-and-ready age of adolescence, she feels that obeying her parents is just too normal, and she wants to explore the beautiful mysteries of adulthood. With an attitude as big as a watermelon, she begins to cross certain thresholds that were established in her home from the time she can first remember.

During these days, many teenagers begin to party, and many form intimate friendships long before they are ready. Others pretend they have experienced the light and glimmer of the adult world to impress their innocent comrades, who often dream of their own special moment to come.

These powerful forces sometimes change teenagers too quickly. Much like an over-ripened fruit that is smelly and unpleasant to be around, their attitude begins to stink. Bad choices turn into mistakes, which later haunt them far into adulthood. Many of these young people eventually come to their senses and find redemption after they have walked down many bumpy roads, but others live with pain and regret for the rest of their lives.

Carissa, the girl in our story, was saved just in time from experiencing the pain of regret over poor choices. She was handpicked specifically by the designer and architect of her soul, the one and only Son of God, who was the only love who could redeem her from the curse and bondage of her corrupted state. Although she was on the road to destruction, He kept His eye on her. Even before she was crafted and shaped in her mother's womb, before she was even thought of, her Savior and Lord had a special plan and purpose for her life. He knew that she had to find Him at just the right time. When that time came, He was there to rescue her from the pitfalls of her lust and selfishness. Before she could cross over into the crushing jaws of the world and its ways, He saved her.

Carissa was a typical teenage girl; she could not wait to see what the world had to offer. Her Heavenly Lover and Redeemer, however, had another plan for her. Jesus was watching out for her, and before she could step over the line to explore the unfamiliar territories of life, He picked her—just in the nick of time.

Carissa's story is familiar to many single Christian girls. The night that changed her life started out like any other Sunday evening. Grandma (also called "Nana") prepared dinner and set the table with her best chinaware from England, as is the custom in many West Indian homes. Carissa always enjoyed her grandmother's rice and peas, the homegrown fried chicken, the macaroni and cheese, and the rum-flavored carrot punch or soursop juice. Nana was the only one Carissa knew who could cook rice and peas with such a unique flare. Carissa would often hide in the kitchen and steal a spoonful before dinner. She loved all the aromas of her grandmother's cooking, and it brought delight to her every Sunday.

However, there was only one drawback, Carissa had to eat the meal at the dining table with her grandparents. This was a problem because they had the bad habit of belching loudly and boisterously, bringing Carissa's desire for food to a sudden halt. To make it worse, she could not excuse herself from the table. She had to consume every bit of the meal because custom dictated that once thanks for the food had been given, you had to eat everything on your plate. After all, many children in India and Africa did not have anything to eat, so you were expected not to waste any food.

That evening, Carissa hurriedly ate dinner before the blast of belching began. Then she ran to her room to read a teenage love story in the latest Mills and Boon book. But her plans were not to be.

In her grandparents' home on Sunday evenings, beautiful music filled the house. The melody of the songs from Jim Reeves and the Gaithers' music brought a soothing lullaby bringing comfort to Carissa's heart.

Though she did not know the Savior at the time, the music always touched her.

This evening was different, though. Carissa settled down in her room to listen to the music and read her novel. She was soon nodding off to sleep. Suddenly, as if from a far distance, she heard Grandma announced, "Carissa, you are going to church with me tonight." Carissa was a bit hesitant, but she knew she had better comply. Her grandmother spoke again, insisting that Carissa was going to the house of the Lord by hook or crook, if necessary.

The stern and determined look on Nana's face drove her into the shower, and in a few minutes, she was ready for church. Under no circumstance could she keep her grandmother waiting. She quickly dressed in a red, long-sleeved linen outfit and put on a lovely pair of black suede shoes. Her Aunt Joy had sent her the attire and shoes from England, and she had little choice but to wear them. Nana thought she looked like a charming young lady, but in Carissa's mind, she looked more like a little old lady. She hoped the boys who played soccer in the streets would not see her going to church with the older woman. To add insult to injury, she was wearing a long-sleeved dress on a sweltering summer day.

Carissa walked through the door of the church and made her way to the back. That way she could bolt like lightning once the service was over. Attendance was a bit scanty on that Sunday night. There were only a few senior saints and a handful of young people.

As Carissa and Grandma took their seats, they were greeted with warm handshakes and smiles from the members who sat next to them. One girl grabbed Carissa's attention. She was short and cute and wore a yellow summer dress. The radiant smile on her face and the beam in her eyes attracted

Carissa's attention. "What is she so happy about?" Carissa muttered under her breath.

The girl was about the same age as Carissa, which made her even more curious. She could not take her eyes off her. The young lady stood alone with a hand raised to the sky. She had no shame as she sang the chorus:

> Majesty, worship His Majesty,
> Unto Jesus, be glory, honor, and praise.
> Majesty, kingdom authority . . .

Wow! Carissa thought, *this girl is about my age, and she is so brave to stand alone and worship before all these people.* This was contrary to what Carissa had always believed. Somehow, in her mind, she had always thought that church was only for the old and dying. Young people had no place there; they needed to enjoy the world. Then, when they were old and gray, they could go to church. But Carissa was enlightened that night. Not only were older folk singing the songs of the Redeemer, but the younger people also were singing, and even louder. And they looked excited, too.

This piqued her interest even more, and she felt like a nervous teenager on her first date. After the singing of the choruses, there were testimonies and ministry in song. As folks made their way to the pulpit, Carissa recognized a different spirit. It was as if a light glowed on their faces as they testified and sang about Jesus. Her uneasiness was apparent as she looked around to see whether anyone was watching her. Her inquisitiveness, however, soon turned to fascination.

Then came the message. Much to her amazement, the sermon about the saving grace of Jesus Christ hit her like a ton of bricks. The young preacher told a story of a lad who left his mother's Christian home and went off to college. During that time, his professors somehow convinced him that God did not exist, so he aborted his Christian teachings and told his mother that he could no longer believe in a God he could not see.

The preacher continued to relay the story of how the young man was on his way back to college from one of his holiday visits when he made the wrong decision to jump cars on a train and fell. He was severely injured and was hospitalized.

As the boy lay in pain in the hospital bed, his mother ministered to him. "Darling, are you feeling pain?" she gently asked.

"Yes, Ma," the boy responded.

"Where is the pain, son? Can you see it?"

"No, Ma, of course not."

With that admittance from her son, the mother plunged in, "You see, my son, the way you can feel the pain, but cannot see it, is the same way I can feel the presence of the Holy Spirit in my heart. Just the way you know the pain is there but cannot see it, that is how I know that my master is walking and talking with me. And He is right here with us tonight."

As the boy observed the joy emanating from his mother's face, heard the way she talked about her Lord, and saw the tears flowing down her cheeks, his heart buckled under conviction. The young man cried out to the Lord for forgiveness for his foolish thoughts and ways.

The preacher culminated his message and gave the altar call. Carissa was trembling like a leaf, feeling as if her heart was changing from a heart of stone to a heart of flesh (similar to the tender chicken she had for dinner). She was under conviction and she knew it, but her heart was as stubborn as a horse. She kept telling herself, *I can do this another day. I am too young to become a Christian; I have time. If I become a Christian, what will my friends think of me when I go to school tomorrow?*

As the congregation rose to sing "I Surrender All," tears began to flow down her cheeks like light rain on a spring leaf, but still she would not yield. The battle of wills began to intensify as she looked around to see who was watching. *Is Grandma staring at me? I don't want her to see me like this. I will never live it down if she finds out I am thinking about her Lord.* After the song, the congregation took their seats and the preacher gave a final appeal.

Carissa felt like she was losing control and as the preacher made his last entreaty, like a streak of lightning, she bolted for the door. A young man saw what was happening and quickly intercepted her. He gently asked if she wanted to give her heart to Christ, and in total acquiescence she said yes. Carissa was counseled by one of the sisters, who used a simple seven-step approach:

Realize that you are a sinner (Romans 3:23; 1 John 1:10).

Realize you cannot save yourself
(John 3:3).

Acknowledge that Jesus came into the world and gave His life to save sinners just like you and me (John 3:16).

You must repent and turn away from sin (Acts 2:38).

You must confess your sins to God, who alone has the power to cleanse you from your sins (1 John 1:9).

You must call upon Jesus Christ in sincere and earnest prayer (Psalm 50:15).

You must believe and by faith receive Jesus so He alone can control your life.

The counseling process lasted about forty-five minutes. Carissa could hear the woman's words, but she wasn't really listening. She sat looking at the woman with the opened Bible in her lap, but in her mind and heart, she had already surrendered.

Yes, Jesus, yes! Carissa repeated in her heart. *I give up. You have been nudging my heart for so long, and tonight I am giving in.*

The tears began to flow like a river as she bowed on her knees. Prompted by the counselor, Carissa prayed aloud, "Jesus, I surrender to You. I want You to be my Lord and Savior. Forgive me for my sins and make me Your child. I confess You as Lord and Savior of my life. I believe that You died on the cross for my sins, and I receive You into my heart."

In total surrender, Carissa turned her life over to the Savior. It was the start of a new path for her, a new relationship, a new way of thinking. She soberly reflected on the verse her counselor left with her, 2 Corinthian 5:17: *Therefore, if anyone is in Christ, the new creation has come: The old has gone, the new is here!* (NIV).

Grandma left for home ahead of Carissa. She wanted to give the counselor enough time to speak with her granddaughter. The older woman had spent hours on her knees crying out to God for this girl, and she wasn't going to let anything spoil the moment of her coming to know the Lord.

That night was a most beautiful night for Carissa. The stars seemed to shine brighter, and the moon looked fuller. It was almost as if the heavenly bodies were walking with her—indeed, as if they were kissing her face. Needless to say, she was excited.

"I did it! I can't believe it. I did it!" she whispered under her breath. She didn't care that the boys who sat on the fence stared at her as if she were a mad woman as she moved her lips in prayer. She was on cloud nine, and she wasn't going to allow anybody or anything to dampen her mood.

That night, after she got home, she could not sleep. She got up and rummaged through a drawer for her grandmother's hymnal and sang, "I Surrender All, "The Old Rugged Cross," "What Can Wash Away My Sins?" and a couple more hymns until sleep cradled her like a baby in its mother's arms.

The next day she felt an exuberant joy she could not explain. She wanted everybody to know about her new love. Her classmates noticed her extremely quiet demeanor and were suspicious.

"What is wrong with you, girl? Why are you smiling to yourself?" one girl inquired.

Carissa had found a man—no, the Man—who knew her before time and space began, the Man who knew her even while she was yet in her mother's womb (Psalm 139). She felt like the woman at the well in John's Gospel, even though she was only fifteen and had not yet been with a man. Like the woman, she felt as if a load had been lifted off her back, and she wanted to tell everybody.

The woman at the well of Samaria had been married five times, and the man she was living with was not her husband. Searching for fulfillment, but unable to find it, she kept changing men in a quest to find satisfaction (John 4). Carissa, on the other hand, was a teenager and had not had the experiences of a grown woman. However, like the woman at the well of Samaria, she was searching for love, fulfillment, and peace. And at the appointed time, Jesus showed up for both of them. He gave them water from the well; that is, the joy that the Holy Spirit gives. That water never dries up, and it always satisfies.

Both Carissa and the Samaritan woman received the gift of the Holy Spirit when they surrendered their lives to Jesus Christ. The woman at the well met Jesus and accepted Him as Lord and Savior. Then the immediate indwelling of the Holy Spirit gave her such joy that she ran to the city and left her water pot behind. She wanted to tell everybody about her salvation experience (see John 4). She could not keep it to herself. It was the same for Carissa.

After surrendering her heart to the Lord, she went to school the next day and began to tell her friends about her newfound friend, Jesus. She wasn't afraid or ashamed of church and Christianity anymore; she wanted the entire school to hear about Him. Some of her friends thought she was a fanatic, but Carissa kept spreading the word nonetheless.

That evening she told her grandfather about her experience. To her surprise, he was a bit skeptical. "I will give you a week to change your mind," he told her. This made her more determined than ever to share her experience, and she began to sing as she washed the dishes, swept the house, and did other chores.

Her grandfather was annoyed by this change in the household. *Another Christian in the house?* he grumbled to himself. He had a strange religion of his own and did not attend church with his wife. He believed in serving his God from home by playing sacred songs on Sundays. He created his own Bible and lived by his own religious rules. Praying and reading the Bible was not his thing, and he would often become extremely upset when Grandma wanted to go to church. She had to get his permission to leave the house, as he was the man of the house and she had to obey him.

But Grandma was not moved. She consistently served her Savior at home and spent countless hours reading the Word on her porch. This left an indelible mark of appreciation for the Word of God on Carissa's mind. Grandma could not attend church on Sunday mornings and was only allowed to go on some Sunday nights. She had to stay home and attend to her "king," the man of the house. She had to attend to her wifely duties instead of going to church and "gossiping with the hypocrites," as her husband's man-made religion put it.

Carissa had always despised her grandfather's ideas and abusive ways. Witnessing his unreasonable demands on her grandmother, she had often hurled insults at him from under her breath. When she became a Christian, however, she had a change of opinion. Her new, regenerated heart no longer exploded with resentment and condemnation. Now it was filled with love and forgiveness for him.

To backtrack a little, it was no ordinary happenstance when Carissa found her Savior. Her life journey was a normal Caribbean one, where both her mother and father went to the United States for a better life and left her behind to live with her grandmother.

When Carissa, at age nine, lost her mother to migration, she had already lost her father, who left the year she was born. Hence, she missed the nurture and warm embrace of her own parents and longed for the day when she could lay eyes on her dad. She wanted him to see how beautiful she was, and she wanted to have the opportunity to sit in his lap and lean on his shoulders.

Years passed, and from time to time she wondered when and how she would meet this missing-in-action dad. When she met Jesus Christ, she knew she had found a real daddy. He told her in His Word that even if father and mother forsook her, He would take her up and hold her close (Psalm 27:10). That promise gave Carissa hope and a new scope on life. As she started growing in grace and knowledge of her Savior and spending more time with Him, the love of her life, she experienced a deep satisfaction and the freedom to call Him "Abba Father" (see John 1:12–13).

Through Jesus, Carissa found a new family, the family of God. She met folks who told her they loved her, who invited her to their homes to sit and dine with them. She had new uncles, daddies, aunties, and sisters. She had new mothers, who taught her the Word and how to groom herself, how to cook, and how to develop newfound talents. She even found brothers, who walked her home after youth fellowship to ensure her safety. Carissa was living a wonderful life until the "frogs" started to show up.

Chapter 3

Carissa Starts to Like Boys

Carissa grew into a devoted Christian teenager. She loved church and was involved in just about every activity created for the youth, whether it was mission trips, youth camps, young people's festivals, drama groups, or house-to-house evangelism. Just name it, and Carissa claimed it as her calling.

She also developed a passion for creative writing in preparation for the youth rally competition. This would later open up doors to minister at open-air campaigns, gospel concerts, and regular church services. She was totally involved in church life.

Despite all her activities, she still harbored a deep longing inside to identify with a family of her own. She passionately desired a family with whom she could share her love and devotion—a family she had never had. Sadly, this search for her Mr. Fabulous would take her to places that she could not ever have imagined.

You may find yourself in a similar situation. You have longed for a family of your own and have grown tired with the waiting. One day you wonder to yourself, *What am I waiting for, when there are so many charming, attractive suitors in the nightclubs and at the baseball games? There are many available men I could take to church, and if I don't take them, who will? I see no harm in dating a man of the world; many of them are more experienced in how to treat a woman, anyway.*

If not nipped in the bud, the compromising thoughts continue and grow stronger: *Look at how they look at me when I walk down the street. I don't get the same attention and compliments at church.* Then a tall, dark, handsome, and well-dressed guy takes you out for coffee—and wow. He is great company and easy to talk to, and he wants to see you again.

This presents a common temptation for many young Christian ladies. They just can't seem to understand why they have to wait so everlasting long. *Will Mr. Fabulous ever show up?* is the question that haunts many women who lie in bed looking at the ceiling night after night.

Meet Danny

Danny was an eye-catcher for the girls at Carissa's church. A man of God and extremely talented, he was tall, dark, and strangely handsome—at least, he was to Carissa. He attended high school with her, and he was very smart. He played the guitar at youth fellowship, and he was also the youth leader at their church and a counselor at their youth camp.

This young man seemed the real deal for all the girls who wanted to marry a pastor. Carissa, like so many others, could not get him out of her mind. She talked, slept, and dreamed about Danny, even at daylight in the midday sun.

The infatuation intensified when Danny began going to Carissa's house on Mondays to assist her with math homework. She couldn't wait for school to end on Mondays because that meant Danny was coming to her house. In fact, she loved Mondays even more than Sundays. During the tutoring sessions, she would see Danny for two to three hours, but math was the last thing on her mind. Of course, she failed the math exam every semester, but Danny would assist her all over again.

Carissa's one-sided secret romance continued for a while until she mustered the courage to write Danny a love letter to express her feelings. Poor Carissa—the disappointment, embarrassment, shame, and pain when she realized that Danny viewed her as only a sister. It took her the rest of her teenage years to get over her broken heart.

The worst part of it was that Danny would often quote a certain Scripture verse in his message to the youth: *Seek ye first the kingdom of God, and His righteousness; and all these things shall be added unto you* (Matthew 6:33 KJV). *Why does he have to use that verse all the time in his messages?* Carissa thought. *I seek the kingdom of God. Why is he being so super-spiritual? I wonder if he is trying to tell me something.*

Carissa's hurt intensified when she discovered that another girl had eyes on Danny. Maria was Carissa's friend and was likewise interested in Danny. She was extremely petite and outgoing, and she dressed in trendy, colorful outfits. Carissa was dejected; she was no match for this girl.

The situation worsened when Carissa learned that Danny had walked Maria to the bus stop after youth fellowship. Carissa loved her friend, but she loved Danny more, so she tried to hide her feelings when the three of them were in the same company.

However, Maria eventually experienced the same fate with Danny as had Carissa. Danny saw her as a sister too, and he was just being kind to the two girls. He wasn't ready for a committed relationship and was only being a supportive friend to both of them.

As the young ladies matured, they realized what was happening and became lifelong friends. They spent weekends at each other's house and became confidantes to the point where they were like blood sisters. Carissa gained a true friend in Maria.

Over the years, Danny became one of Carissa's dearest brothers in the Lord as a result of his continued encouragement and prayers for her. He later married a wonderful young lady who was the perfect match for him. Their music and other outreach ministries impacted many generations of young people for Christ.

Meet Christopher

During that time, Carissa met Christopher. He was pleasing to the eyes, at least to Carissa. He was a muscular young man with a great smile, and he gave a comforting hug. He was madly in love with her.

The two met on a mission's trip. *What better place to meet the man of your dreams?* Carissa thought. The relationship blossomed quickly, and Christopher became her first boyfriend. He brought her flowers and rode his bicycle nearly eight miles every weekend just to see her. Sometimes he would take two and three buses during the week just to see her again, making Carissa feel really special. He often cooked lunch and took it to her job just to surprise her.

Carissa and Christopher spent hours picnicking in the botanical gardens and enjoying their time together. He took her to his youth fellowship to meet his friends, and she also met his mother, brother, and even his coworkers. He was the guy who taught her how to kiss, and she was really in love with him—until he bought a ring. At this juncture of Carissa's life journey, she was preparing for college, but Christopher was on a mission to get married.

It was Christmas Eve, and they had gone to the ice-cream garden for their regular evening stroll. It was her favorite love nest. In the winter months, the beautiful lawn was green and luscious, and daffodils and dandelions bloomed in the middle of an island of white painted stones. The water fountains with their blue and yellow bulbs lent a unique romantic charm to the garden. Lovers swarmed the place, walking and holding hands, blushing at the whisper and chatter of love.

In their visits to the garden, Christopher and Carissa often hid away under park benches with their bodies touching as they gazed deeply into each other's eyes. Large trees overarched the benches and provided cool shade on many hot humid days. It was as if time did not exist for them. This evening was different, however.

Christopher looked a bit nervous as he handed Carissa her two-scoop ice-cream cone. Before she could take her first taste, Christopher's three scoops fell off his cone, and she noticed he was sweating profusely.

What is wrong with him this evening? Carissa thought. *I wonder if he needs to use the restroom.* Carissa was concerned, but to avoid embarrassing Christopher, she kept her thoughts to herself and began chattering away like a parrot looking at its reflection in the mirror.

Then Christopher did the unthinkable. He went down on his knee and pulled out a little red box from his pocket. Carissa was nervous. *No, no, no!* she screamed silently. *Don't do it. I am not ready for that yet!*

Christopher, oblivious to the fear in Carissa's heart, quickly spoke the dreaded words, "Will you marry me?"

Her heart pounded and skipped a beat, and she knew she had to think quickly. One thing for sure, she wasn't going to break his heart or cause him shame. "Let me think about it," she responded. "Give me a couple of weeks, and I will get back to you."

Christopher was somewhat troubled by her answer, but it was better than hearing "no." He accompanied her home that night, but deep down in the depths of his heart, he knew something wasn't right.

Carissa hid the ring in a dresser drawer. She had told Christopher that she wanted some time to pray, and that was when the trouble began. There was no peace for Carissa; it was almost as if the ring was an omen warning against Christopher's plan. For days, she could not sleep. One night she dreamed there was a hole in the middle of Christopher's church, and it was covered with newspaper. She had nightmares that the ring was broken in two, and in another dream, a pastor told her that the man was not for her.

One night Carissa dreamed that Christopher took her to the beach, where they saw something that looked like a row of spikes in the water. It was three men in white cloaks standing on the water. She could not distinguish one person from the other, and as she and Christopher approached, the men cautioned them in a commanding tone, "When you get to the bottom of this beach, you will see fruit of all kinds, but do not touch them!"

As the two made their way down, they were delighted with the oasis of fruit. Grapes were bundled with apples, pineapples, mangoes, and oranges. Pomegranates, melons, guineps, and a host of other tropical fruits abounded. The scene was tempting, but Carissa remembered the warning from the men and stayed away. Christopher, however, could not resist. He began to pick the fruit, as if he were a tasting expert.

Alarmed, Carissa questioned him. "Christopher, why are you picking the fruit? Remember the warning from the men?"

"Nobody will find out," he said, trying to convince her.

With that Carissa awoke from her sleep and knew she could not marry him. Tormented, she went for counseling. Finally, however, she knew she had to give him the verdict.

"Christopher, I have something to tell you," she began. His heart began to pound, and by the look on Carissa's face, he sensed it wasn't good news. "You see, Christopher, I have been praying for some time about us, and based on the evidence I have seen, and the prompting of the Holy Spirit, I don't believe we should get married at this time."

Christopher was devastated. He cried, but Carissa cried even more. She was heartbroken that she had to break the heart of such a phenomenal guy who was madly in love with her. However, she could not continue to ignore the nudging of the Holy Spirit. Furthermore, her friends were uncomfortable with the relationship, her family members were uneasy about it, and her pastor didn't believe Christopher was the one. A big part of Carissa wanted to hold on to the relationship, but she knew it was better to obey God.

Christopher's friends and family were saddened for him. A few were upset about

Carissa's decision and pledged never to speak to her again. Meanwhile, Christopher moved on. He found a beautiful girl who was crazy about him. Within a year, they were married. Mission accomplished for Christopher.

Carissa was surprised and a little hurt that he moved on so quickly, but she wished him well. She consoled herself that she had done the right thing in obeying her Lord.

CHAPTER 4

Has God Forgotten?

Normally we expect a bonus after we have put in a lot of overtime and exceeded our job's expectation. Children often expect a reward after they do all their chores, especially if they have gone the extra mile. It is the same with us as Christians.

We often anticipate the Lord will bless us more because we have obeyed Him all our lives. We watch others walk in disobedience and expect that their lives will not turn out as well as ours. However, that is not always the case. Sometimes we look in amazement at how well their lives have turned out, even after they have failed the Lord time and time again. We are tempted to wonder if maybe we should have done things our way in the first place.

Take, for example, the Prodigal Son's older brother. Imagine what it must have been like when his younger brother requested his inheritance and ran off to live an extravagant lifestyle, while he stayed behind and remained faithful to their father. Stretch your imagination a bit and think of the many nights he must have heard his father lamenting for his lost son, while he, the older brother, lay in bed and wished his father would just forget about the wild and ungrateful boy.

Imagine how he faithfully served and consoled his father during the younger brother's absence. Imagine how he carefully attended to his father's estate to ensure that he wasn't taken advantage of, and how he dutifully supervised the servants, hoping to make his father proud of him.

Then the unimaginable happened; his wayward brother returned home. How startled he must have been as he watched the jubilation, the celebration, and the forgiveness his father extended to this runaway. *How could this happen? I have been faithful to my father all this time, and he never had a party for me*, he fumed. The jealousy and the anger must have consumed him to the point where he could not withhold his feelings. Speaking up, he complained, "Dad, I have been here all this time, and I have never left your side. But as soon as this scoundrel returns, you are acting like he is the cat's pajamas. What is wrong with you, Dad?" (see Luke 15).

This kind of feelings of betrayal are common for many Christian young ladies who have waited for the Lord and lived in obedience to Him. They save themselves for marriage, live faithful Christian lives, attend church regularly, and read the Bible more than the average person. Despite their stellar lives, however, they spend countless nights on their knees appealing to the Lord to bless them with Mr. Fabulous, but to no avail.

They often wonder if the Lord has forgotten them, or maybe they have inherited some type of generational curse. Some well-meaning Christian friend invites them to an intercessory prayer meeting and lays hands on them, asking the Lord to deliver them from this curse, but nothing seems to change. The frustration and abandonment continue to suck the very life out of them.

Carissa Struggles with Loneliness

Carissa felt like the Prodigal Son's older brother. She had obeyed the Lord in letting go of Christopher and believed that her Mr. Fabulous would show up. Sadly, that was not the case.

Her three years of college were extremely lonely without Christopher around to pamper her. She had no visitors showing up for her in the school's lobby, like her college mates did. Though her focus was set on completing her studies, there were times she wished she had a visitor who would bring her goodies and flowers, and even take her out on Saturday evenings when she needed a break.

One year turned into three, and Carissa was still praying. She was fully involved in her school's Christian club and mission's ministry, and she committed all her summer vacations to Bible- camp outreach programs. Nonetheless, the loneliness did not abate. She longed for a husband who would provide the security she had never received from her parents as a young girl.

There were days when Carissa did not know how she would come up with money for the next college fee or for food to eat. She had to trust the Lord one day at a time. This taught her the valuable lesson that the Lord's promises were sure. He told her in His Word that even if her mother and father forsook her, He would take her up (see Psalm 27:10). Throughout her college years, Carissa lived believing in this promise.

Carissa had to trust the Lord for everything. There were times when she did not have the college fee at the beginning of the school year, and the Lord would provide it just in the nick of time. At the moment when she needed to sign up for her dorm and get her keys, the money would be there. There were days when she could not find the money for books, and God would provide the money just before class started.

One day as Carissa was in class, she became anxious as she realized that she did not have the money for dinner that evening. It was approaching four o'clock, and she would soon have to retire to her dorm without dinner or money to buy even a snack.

On her way back to her room, Carissa began to pray silently, *Lord Jesus, your Daughter is here again. Please provide something for me to eat. You promise in Your Word that you will never leave me nor forsake me, so Lord, I am looking to You again.*

As Carissa approached the door, she heard the phone in her suite ringing. It was a call for her to attend to a visitor in the lobby. As she entered the visitors' area, she was greeted by a woman from her church. She had a grocery bag filled with everything Carissa needed or wanted. Soap, snacks, milk, you name it—it was there in the bag. Carissa could not believe it. The Lord had answered her prayer before she even asked it.

Another time Carissa was in bed praying when she heard a knock at her window. It was her friend Antoinette, and she was hungry. Antoinette asked if Carissa had money, because she wanted to buy food from the snack shop. Carissa only had a

$1.50 and did not know how she would find dinner for herself. Nonetheless, she opened the window and gave Antoinette everything she had, trusting that the Lord would provide double for her.

Exactly an hour later, there was another knock on her window. This time it was a friend with an envelope for her. One of Carissa's friends had sent her a hundred dollars. The Lord blew her mind again. Then and there, it was confirmed in her mind that her Savior could be trusted.

Throughout college Carissa continued to experience the Lord's favor on her life. In fact, it was so evident that her friends would often say, "Girl, the Lord really loves you!" She often used this opportunity to share with them how the Lord had told her at her conversion that He would take up for her and provide for her, even though her mother and father were not present.

Although Carissa was experiencing the Lord's provision in supernatural ways, she was still lonely. She wanted to find her Mr. Fabulous, just like everyone else. She wanted to have her own family.

Meet Rick

After graduation, Carissa moved to another church closer to where she lived. This is where she met Rick. He was different from any other guy she had ever known.

Rick had a handsome face and an athletic physique. He was deeply committed to the things of the Lord, and he was also a great listener. He took Carissa anywhere she wanted to go. He would pick her up and then drive her home from church. He would drive her to work in the morning and make arrangements to pick her up at the end of the day.

To Carissa, he was her knight in shining armor, and she was smitten. He had all the qualities she was looking for in a man. They could talk for hours about the things of the Lord. Furthermore, he was a gentleman and pleasing to the eyes. Her grandmother loved him, her pastor was pleased with the relationship, and her friends thought they made a great match. Carissa was the live bug and kept him laughing. Rick was the controlled one and an attentive listener. As she talked for hours about her challenges and blessings, he would look into her eyes and ask all the right questions at just the right time. On top of all that, he was an excellent kisser.

Carissa felt sure he was the one until the unthinkable happened—he wanted out. It was a Sunday evening. He drove her home as usual, and they were sitting in the car having their usual evening chat when he announced that he had something to tell her.

"Carissa, I am rethinking our relationship," he said. "Fifty percent of me wants to be married, but the other fifty wants to remain single. I don't know how long it will last, but this is how I am feeling right now, and I can't seem to shake it."

Carissa was devastated. "Well, if that is how you feel, I don't want somebody who is not entirely ready for marriage," she replied calmly. But inside, her heart was breaking.

"It is not you; it is me," Rick apologized.

Carissa hated that line; it was just a familiar line from guys who really wanted to break up. Her world had been turned upside down, and now she would have to wait again.

Where is God? she thought. *Why is He allowing me to experience this? I really believed that Rick was the one for me.* Carissa went to bed feeling rejected and dejected.

Weeks, months, years passed, and she still could not shake Rick. It was as if she were living a nightmare. At one point, her friends wondered if she was obsessed. She would talk about Rick all the time. It did not matter what the conversation was about; Carissa would somehow include Rick in the mix.

They continued as friends, but Carissa secretly hoped for the day when Rick would change his mind. As time went on, she complained to the Lord, *why am I waiting so long, Lord? Wait for what?*

Eventually, Carissa began to make peace with the situation. She found a new focus. Her quest for ministry and her love for the Lord led her to sign up for Bible school. Carissa firmly believed that this pull to pursue a degree in counseling and psychology would open doors for her to minister to others and would provide opportunities to share her faith and experiences with the younger women in her circle. Carissa felt that she had a message to pass on to those who came behind her.

Bible school was a most exciting experience for her. She loved the counseling courses and enjoyed classroom debates about the Word of God. She made many Christian friends who had a similar passion for the things of the Lord. During those three years, the Lord did a wonderful thing in Carissa's life. He opened avenues for her to talk about the hurts she had experienced as a child who did not have her mother and father around to nurture her.

It was easy for her to divulge the intimate details of her life in the safe environment of the school. Other students had experienced similar childhood traumas, and they would share and pray, cry and hug, laugh and eat the Word together. The tissue box was a frequent companion as tears flowed like a river and the wounds of the heart began to mend. Dead hope sprang to life again as the Lord reminded the students that He came to heal the brokenhearted and bind up their wounds (see Psalm 147:3). The camaraderie was just what she needed, and for one of the few times in her life, she felt secure.

During this time, Carissa was able to unearth some of the things that had been buried in the back of her mind for as long as she could remember. There were nights when she would lay in bed in tears, remembering the loneliness and rejection she had felt as a child not having a mother and father in her life. There were times when her pillow was soaked as she remembered the unfair treatment meted out to her because her mom and dad were not there to protect her. As painful as the memories were, it was good to recall them. God was pouring out the oil of healing on her very being, and she felt as if a big load was being pulled off her back.

Hearing about the experiences of others helped Carissa learn how to forgive. She learned how to move forward by making peace with her past, and this marked a new beginning for her.

Chapter 5

Life's Twists and Turns

Life's twists and turns are mostly unpredictable
Like a paradox leaving you tossing in bed or sleeping like a log
Some days, seem like thunder and lightening
While, in other days, the skies inhabit the delightful presence of the rainbow.

Many days come with praise and worship
While others are perplexed with questions and wonders

At times, the pocket is empty and
filled with holes
And other times, the reservoir over-
flows in an abundance of wealth.

Some days the doctors give a clean
bill of health
And other days, they confound you
with the news of death
One day may have a belly full
of laughter
While others are filled with deep
sorrow and pain.

Life's twists and turns then, leaves
a lingering question… Who is
in charge?

Meet the Family

Carissa moved to New York City after finishing Bible school. She landed a new teaching job, made new friends, and found a new church. It was an excellent opportunity to start her life afresh. To top it off, she was now living in the same country as her mother and father. She would get to meet her sisters, one brother, and a host of other family members she had longed to meet all her life.

Shortly after her arrival, she found a familiar church that held similar beliefs as her previous meeting place. Carissa felt welcomed, and the folks seemed like family. The aunt that she stayed with was a Christian, as was her mother, who lived close to the aunt's home.

The new job was somewhat challenging and stressful, but Carissa had enthusiastic and supportive friends who would pick her up for church, take her out for supper, and even visit and pray with her. She joined a young women's ministry group composed of likeminded women. This group was just what she needed at the time, as she had recently completed Bible school and had much to share at the group's book clubs, retreats, and Bible studies. She received tremendous support from this ministry as well. She was assigned a mentor who prayed with her on weekdays, and Carissa mentored others as well. It was a give-and-take situation, and she felt a true sense of contentment and belonging.

It was at this time that Carissa finally met her dad. To backtrack a bit, Carissa met her father within the second week of her arrival in the United States. The new job provided lodging at a hotel in the city for two weeks, with the understanding that within that time, she would find permanent accommodations.

Carissa called her Aunt Cutie, who lived in one of the suburbs close to Carissa's job, and Aunt Cutie agreed to take her in. Carissa felt doubly blessed by this arrangement, as the church was only five minutes away from the house. It felt as if she had walked through a clearly open door.

Everything was working out for her. It became even clearer to Carissa that the Lord was leading her steps when her Aunt Cutie said that she had a number for Carissa's dad. She was ecstatic. Her dream of meeting her dad was about to unfold, and she wouldn't miss it for the world.

The next day was a very busy day for Carissa. She was scheduled for her job orientation and training, but during a short break, she called her dad. He seemed genuinely enthusiastic to meet her. Carissa was pleased with the Lord. *Lord, you are surely working out things for my good,* she prayed. *I can finally see what You have been doing all along.*

It was a strange experience as she talked with her father for the first time. She did not know whether she should feel excited, nervous, or scared; she was at a strange place emotionally. But she did know she had to put on her big-girl skirt and face the music.

Carissa told her father that she was staying at the hotel just across the street from where he worked. They arranged to meet in the lobby of the hotel. "Do you need to know what I am wearing?" Carissa asked.

"No, I will know my child when I see her," he replied.

As Carissa entered the lobby, a tall, handsome, and stately man walked over and hugged her. It was love at first sight, and Carissa was elated. The long-awaited encounter had finally come to pass.

Mr. Peyton, her father, took her to one of the finest Italian restaurants in the city. After chitchatting a bit and catching up on the reason for Carissa's migration, her dad said the most honorable and amazing thing any child, who has felt abandoned their entire life, needs to hear.

"Carissa," he said, "I have made some mistakes in my life. Leaving you at a tender age was one of the worst things a man could ever do. Please forgive me. I will spend the rest of my life making it up to you."

Those words brought true healing. Carissa felt a deep sense of peace as she forgave her daddy, the man she had always been angry with but longed to meet, the man whom she had never seen but felt a sense of connection with. I know it sounds like a fairy-tale ending, but when God is working out His providential purpose for a person's life, the story is often incredible and mind-boggling.

You see, my friends, "for such a time as this" is one of the most common phrases heard from the lips of people who waited for the Lord to work and could not understand why He was taking so long, but then the twists and turns of their lives eventually proved to be more remarkable than they could ever have imagined. "Why wait?" was their cry during all those years. But God is always on time. He works out His purposes in ways we do not understand, and His timing perfectly fits together the puzzles of life.

The Bible story of Esther portrays a young woman who was left with her cousin Mordecai to raise her. As I stretch my imagination a bit, I imagine she must have felt a sense of emptiness at not having her own parents to nurture and raise her. God, however, had a specific path for Esther that she could not even imagine as she grew up in her cousin's care.

As Esther grew into a beautiful young woman, she must have wondered why she had to wait to marry one of the many Jewish boys. Little did she know that God had a specific, unique, "Esther only" plan for her. Just think how strange it must have seemed when she was selected as one of the virgins who would prepare themselves as a potential bride for the king.

Esther probably felt she was no match for the other girls, who likely were wealthier, of more noble descent, and more experienced in the ins and outs of palace living. But God! He selected Esther for "such a time as this" to become the queen of one of the most famous and powerful kings of the time.

Now, Carissa's story, in regard to meeting her father, was certainly different from Esther's. However, it is likely that both missed the presence of their parents in their growing-up years. As Carissa reflected on her childhood longing to meet her father, she remembered all the times she had questioned God, "God, why do I have to have two missing parents? Many kids live with at least one parent, but both of mine are missing."

She recalled the many times she had cried on her birthday, Christmas, Mother's Day, and Father's Day because she wanted to be like the other kids who knew the security of growing up with their parents. Her grandmother provided a stable home and taught her the ways of the Lord, but how Carissa longed for her own parents. That emptiness could not be filled by anyone else, but the ones who had given birth to her—or so she thought.

At this juncture in her life, she recalled the days when she had refused to eat at the dinner table with her grandparents. "What is wrong with you, child?" her grandmother would inquire.

"I want my mother," she would lament. But Carissa had to dry her tears and push forward, the realization dawning that there was no one to rescue her.

To her surprise, when she finally met her parents, she discovered that they were very different from her grandmother. As their lives unfolded before her, she recognized they had been in no position to raise her. In the days ahead, God would use her to support and encourage them.

Carissa's mom, Tina, was a Christian; however, she was broken and needed a tremendous amount of healing from her past mistakes. Tina was a beautiful woman with a bright smile. She had a magnetic personality that pulled others to her, and she exhibited beautiful and classy taste in her dress. Nonetheless, mountains of regret haunted her at night.

Carissa had forgiven Tina for leaving her at the age of nine, but her mother could not shake the pain of being unable to turn back the hands of time. Tina would often call Carissa at night, and even in the early morning, just to relive the *why*s and *if*s of her life. This was extremely stressful for Carissa, but she tried to assure her mom of the power of self-forgiveness and the healing it can bring. She had to repeat this over and over until Tina finally learned to live with her mistakes.

On the other hand, Carissa's father, Mr. Peyton, was doing the best he could in the situation. He continued to meet with Carissa for lunch and gave her a helping hand when she needed a door fixed, a computer repaired, or just a shoulder to lean on.

Carissa was comforted to have her parents in her life. Her longing was finally realized, and she felt a sense of belonging. She shared her faith with them, sharing how the Lord's grace and mercy had taken her through the ups and downs of her childhood struggles. She related how it had seemed as if the Lord was physically present in her college days, protecting her from abuse and misfortune. Through Jesus, she had developed a father-and- daughter relationship with God that was so real, it was almost as if she could touch His face.

Tina was encouraged to hear Carissa's story and proud to learn of the bond between her daughter and Jesus. Tina spent hours reminiscing about her own childhood, wishing she had held on to Jesus the way Carissa had.

Sharing her faith with her family was exciting for Carissa. They often called and asked her to pray for them in the face of challenges or dangers. Mr. Peyton even allowed her to minister at his mother's funeral. Carissa was overjoyed to finally have the chance to tell her patriarchal family about the love of Jesus and how He died to save them from the curse of sin. Her family was receptive and appreciated her faith, but her dad was stubborn.

He would often debate the whole concept of Christianity with Carissa at lunch, dinner, or on long drives to the country area where he lived. Carissa was staunch in her beliefs, and he was adamant that her faith was false. He said she had been brainwashed by the white man, who had taken religion to the Caribbean people after slavery was abolished. He was not going to let that happen to him, he insisted.

Undeterred by her father's resistance, Carissa shared with him how the Lord had showed up in her life at the tender age of fifteen. The relationship was not a natural one, but more like a mystery, she explained. She shared with Mr. Peyton how the Lord revealed Himself to her when she said yes to Him, and how her life was transformed from a little girl who felt lost and abandoned to a girl who had a joy so deep she could not keep it to herself. The mystery of salvation cannot be reasoned or debated, she explained further, but it is a work done in the heart by the Holy Spirit when a person surrenders to the lordship of Jesus Christ.

Mr. Peyton, however, was a tough nut to crack. He could not seem to grasp how a God who loved the world could also condemn a person to hell and doom, or allow so much suffering. "It is the white man's plot to keep us under bondage" was his conclusion to the matter, so Carissa kept praying.

This was often the nature of the conversation between them for the next twelve years. She always looked forward to talking to her dad, regarding it her mission to encourage him to surrender his life to Jesus. The vision to pray for her parents' salvation had started when Carissa met the Lord at fifteen, and she had prayed for them night and day. She was convinced that the Lord had reunited her with her parents for the sole purpose of winning them to the Lord, but little did she know that the purpose was much bigger than she could even think or imagine.

One fateful Christmas, Mr. Peyton complained to Carissa about a pain in his back and lower abdomen. "Go to the doctor," she encouraged him. Weeks dragged into months, and the doctors could not determine what was wrong with him. He took a host of healing herbs, but to no avail. The pain lingered and worsened.

After the doctors finally decided to take a CAT scan, he was diagnosed with pancreatic cancer. He called Carissa on the phone as she traveled home from a vacation at her mother's home and broke the devastating news. Carissa was calm at first. Then she went online to read the prognosis for such a disease. Tears welled up in her eyes when she failed to find any positive information on stage 4 pancreatic cancer. She moved from site to site, but could find no actual source of comfort, and the tears began to surge.

As she boarded the plane, she was prayerful but scared. Could this mean she was going to lose her father? She had known him for ten years and was not ready to give him up. To intensify the situation, he did not know the Lord as his Savior.

Carissa was broken. She could not save him from this dreadful disease, and she could not save him from the terrible nature of sin. "God!" she cried. "Please, save him,

Lord! Save my dad—just for my sake, Lord, please. I am not ready to lose him yet. Lord, I am just getting to know him. Who will walk me down the aisle, if You take him now? Who will fix my car or the lock on my door?" Carissa lamented.

After a brief and emotional breakdown, she pulled herself together and called her father. Her intent was to tell him of the healing power of the Lord. Her mission had another purpose; she wanted to make sure he accepted the Lord, just in case he did not win the battle against this dreadful disease. At first, he was receptive, but it was a long and challenging battle as she watched him move from denial, to hope, to anger, to fear. It was hard.

Chapter 6

Life's Uncertainties

Waiting—is this a new form of pain? It is like a foreign object that cannot be controlled. It releases from your hand as the wind blows, and it sails across the lawn. And you have no say or control as to where it will land.

The wait for healing is like an unpredictable storm that leaves you wondering whether you should go to sleep or stay awake through the night. You are constantly looking to see whether the wind will blow in your direction. The uncertainty of a life-threatening disease can potentially tear your world apart, disrupt your routine, keep you awake at night, and make you tired and helpless.

"Wait for what?" you ask. To see whether your loved one will survive? To see whether God is going to turn you down, while you spend all your resources on medicine and hospital bills? Both unbelievers and Christians struggle with this human fear. In such situations, hope is sometimes found only after a family has explored all human wisdom and turns to God as a last resort.

Does God understand our suffering? Does He know the pain we feel? Does He care? The words from a popular song Does Jesus Care? "Does Jesus care when our heart is sad? Oh yes, He cares; I know He cares," reassures our hearts as we wait and cry and pray.

This was the beginning of a new chapter in Carissa's life. She endured two years of pain and frustration as she watched her dad's personal and physical well-being deteriorate. It was no easy emotional and physical journey, but Carissa took long visits on the weekends to see him.

Oftentimes he wasn't able to talk with her, and there were times when he was angry. Other times he was hopeful and demonstrated a fighting attitude, but the sickness was always a force to be reckoned with. Carissa watched him suffer. She prayed with and for him, and she cried with and for him.

The uncertainty of her dad's condition led to many sleepless and restless nights. This was a tough disease that seemed to squelch the hope of even the brightest and best surgeons around the world. The median survival of this illness is about five months, but months turned into a year, and Carissa's father was still fighting.

The Wait for Healing

At the time of his diagnosis, Mr. Peyton was in great shape. He had just started a new job, and life had taken a wonderful turn for him. Or so he thought, until that tragic diagnosis. He was not ready to let go of life, so he put up a valiant fight. The many and varied surgeries left him weak and in much pain. His wife, Nina, was at his side all the time and made sure he had the necessary medicine and care. There were days when he was bright and cheerful and other days when he would not even look up or talk because of the immense pain.

The visits with her father eventually became unbearable for Carissa. Feeling helpless, she would sing, pray, and minister to him from the Word about the saving grace of Jesus. One day she asked one of her pastors to accompany her to have a talk with her dad. Mr. Peyton was somewhat receptive, but he continued to debate the process of salvation.

The pastor did his best to make pure and straightforward the gospel, but Mr. Peyton resisted. This baffled Carissa, to think a man who was on his sickbed had such a hard time accepting the gospel. She had to remind herself that God is the one who does the saving. All that He asks of us is to go tell, so she continued to pray and preach.

During one of the visits with the pastor present, it seemed as if her dad was close to accepting Jesus as his Lord. But then, Carissa was shattered to hear him say, "I am not ready." She felt like someone had struck her across her face. *How can he be so stubborn?* she thought. By this time, the cancer seemed to have eaten all his flesh and he was down to mere skin and bones. Still, he remained as stubborn as a horse. *God does the saving; you do the telling,* the Holy Spirit reminded her. So, she shared and she prayed.

On a holiday weekend Carissa was on vacation near her dad's home. She decided to stop by for a visit on her way home. Mr. Peyton was up and about; he was even walking. He was extremely happy to see Carissa, and she was delighted to see him. The family decided to play a game of dominos. Mr. Peyton was extremely competitive. Carissa lost all the rounds, but she was happy and hopeful because he was in a robust mood.

Then trouble struck. Carissa and her dad had a disagreement about a family member and he became extremely hostile. He had a meltdown. Carissa was devastated because then and there she realized that she did not really understand him and had not totally forgiven him for all the years when he was absent in her life.

This was a critical time of reckoning for father and daughter. As she listened to him scold her about the need to be there for family, she grew livid, which was unlike her. Mr. Peyton was crying, but Carissa didn't feel sorry for him or even cared. She was defiant. As she watched him cry, her mind was silently railing against him. *You can cry, but where were you when I needed you? Where were you all those years when I cried as a little girl? Where was "family" then? You are not going to put me on a guilt trip—no way—so you can cry as much as you want.* Carissa was cold.

Her father soon realized what he had done and later apologized. However, it seemed as if the feeling of resentment had surfaced like a shark from the ocean and Carissa was angry. *Family? Where was family when I needed them?* The bitter thoughts continued to run through her mind unabated. The apology did nothing to cause her anger to subside. It took her weeks to come to grips with the situation.

The experience taught her a valuable lesson, nonetheless. A person can say they have forgiven, but when the rubber meets the road, they will discover whether they truly have forgiven those who have hurt them. Carissa thought she had put her childhood pain behind her, but she was surprised to realize that she had so many pent-up emotions that needed healing.

Saying "I forgive you" is easy, but true forgiveness does not remind the person of the wrong they have done. True forgiveness does not forget, but neither does it relive the wrong or bury it. It must come to the surface. It is a necessary hurt, and the pain must be carefully and thoroughly addressed.

There are times when a loved one has hurt you and you bury the pain deep in your heart for years. Then a situation arises and the buried pain surges to the surface like water that has lain dormant for many years. As it gushes to the surface, it breaks out in a storm and wreaks devastation. This can tear families apart if not dealt with carefully and prayerfully.

Carissa had to face her pain and acknowledge that she was hurt. She was upset with her parents; however, she had to set them free from what she thought they owed her. No more debt—they could walk free. The healing would take time, but she had to let the bitterness go and set her parents free. Her adult choices were up to her. She had no one to blame but herself. Her parents had made their choices, and she had to make hers, with the leading and courage that the Lord gave her.

She had to set herself free from the past, if she wanted to live an emotionally healthy life. She was ready to do that. After weeks of praying, she was finally able to put the past behind her. God had allowed that situation with her dad to unfold that evening just to teach her the way of forgiveness.

Another year passed and Mr. Peyton was still breathing. He was now down to IVs and bedpans. Apparently, this was it. He was losing the battle, but he wasn't willing to give up the fight for survival. He would continue to do so until his last breath.

During his final days, Mr. Peyton would often call for Carissa to visit him. Whenever she could not go, he was disappointed. She was not comfortable driving the highways and byways alone and had to find someone who could drive her. There were times when no one was available.

When she did visit, her dad was always happy to see her and he would use the opportunity to tell her again that he loved her and was sorry he had not been there for her. At those times, she recognized the Lord had divinely and purposefully arranged the visit just so she could get the healing she needed.

What an awesome and wise God we serve. He can look within the depths of our hearts and recognize the things we need, even when we do not know them ourselves. What an all-wise God He is. He, the Holy Spirit, searches all things, even the deep things of God (see 1 Corinthians 2:10). Who but God could know what Carissa needed? He used her dad's sickness to bring her healing. He earnestly wanted to save her father as well. However, Mr. Peyton had to have a willing heart and Carissa, too, had to have a willing heart to forgive.

Two years passed and Mr. Peyton was taking his last breath. It was a Sunday evening and he wanted her to stay with him. Carissa was afraid, realizing that he could go at any moment. She did not think she could live with the memory of watching her father's passing; it was too painful. Nevertheless, she timidly consented to stay the night. The evening turned to midnight and midnight turned to dawn. Carissa got very little sleep. All night long she was terrified. *What will I do if he passes in the night?* kept running through her mind.

Morning came and Mr. Peyton's faculties began to shut down. He could not move his feet and he was thirsty. "Carissa, help me!" he cried.

"Dad, call out to Jesus. He is right here," she encouraged. He nodded, as if in agreement, and she hoped that he had accepted her Savior.

Carissa prayed and cried. She hoped with all her heart that the Lord had performed the miracle of salvation for her father. Mr. Peyton was traveling the road of death and there was nothing she could do about it. It was too difficult to watch.

This was Carissa's chance to leave. She bolted through the door like a bird escaping from an overnight cave. About two hours after reaching home, the call came. He was gone—her dad was gone.

Carissa was numb. She could not cry anymore. The fear had subsided and the pain was gone. However, she agonized. Did he know Jesus? Was it too late for him?

Her dad was cremated. Carissa sat at the front of the funeral home in wonder at the finality of it all. Psalm 89:48 ran through her mind: *Who can live and not see death, or who can escape the power of the grave?*

Death seems so final, or so we think. But it is not final because one day we will see the

Lord Jesus Christ, whether we have lived for Him or lived as an enemy of the cross (see Luke 16:22; 2 Corinthians 5:6–8). The life we live on earth determines our destiny in eternity. We cannot escape it.

Carissa was satisfied. She had met her dad and forgiven him. The Lord had providentially orchestrated her life and she was content. She had been given the opportunity to share her faith with him and she had done so. "Go tell," the Scriptures say and that she had done. The rest was between her dad and the Lord. She was at peace.

Carissa knew she had to move forward. The rest of her family needed to know the Lord. She had to capitalize on the opportunity to minister to her friends and relatives and the host of coworkers who had come to bid her father farewell. As she rose to the podium to give her tribute, she was ready. It was a memoir about her dad. The child who had not known him for most of her life had something to say.

In her eulogy, Carissa recaptured the first time she met her dad and how elated she felt. She recalled the times when they debated about the Lord around the dinner and lunch tables. She remembered the times when she rested her head on his shoulder and they cried together. It seemed like she had known him all her life, though in reality it was only twelve short years. It was a beautiful story of redemption.

At "such a time as this," God healed and brought life to the dry bones in Carissa's life. Through her pain and suffering came healing and forgiveness. Through her wait and frustration came a new beginning, where she could bring light to a family who knew only darkness.

At "such a time as this," Queen Esther had no clue that God would providentially place her in the kingdom of King Ahasuerus

(Xerxes) to save her people, the Jews, from the jealous wrath of Haman. Haman was on a mission to eradicate the Jewish people from the country of Persia, but God would not allow it. He orchestrated the footsteps of Esther in order to save them.

Haman maliciously put his plan in motion to slaughter the Jewish people, but Esther was in a position to rescue them. She was the queen, but unknown to Haman and others, she was also a Jew. Esther then approached the king and received his favor. As a result, she was able to thwart Haman's intentional plan to "ethnic cleanse" Persia of all the Jews.

God gave Queen Esther the favor she needed with the king long before she was even born. God prepared her heart and trained her to have the right disposition. The breaking, molding, and refining took place long before she met the king. Then, at the appointed time, she rose up and accepted her position as the woman for the job. When the king, from Esther, learned of Haman's plot, the evil manipulator suffered the fate he had planned for the Jewish people. Esther's mission was complete.

This was the purpose and destiny that God had prepared her for all her life. At "such a time as this" Esther had her answer to the question, *wait for what?* Although Carissa's story was by no means similar to Esther's, we can fairly say that both women lived out a purpose that God had designed for them long before they could even think of it or imagine the work He could do through their obedient lives.

CHAPTER 7

Is This Wait Too Long?

We spend most of our lives waiting. A woman may wait for years to find a partner. Then she waits for a baby, and sometimes she has to wait until her husband decides which house they will buy. Then she waits again as her children grow up and finally go away to college, so that she can afford some free time for herself.

Later she finds she is waiting for retirement. Then oops—she is in retirement and realizes that she is waiting to die from a terminal illness. The next thing you know, she comes to the striking realization that all her life was taken up with waiting for an event to happen, and in the process, she forgot to live.

Abraham and Sarah waited for a son for many years, until they were past the prime of their lives (see Genesis). In tears, Hannah waited for a son as she faced humiliation and ostracism from her husband's other wife. Samson waited to avenge himself for what the Philistines had done to him and Israel, and he paid the ultimate sacrifice. Ruth waited for Boaz to make a decision about their future as she continued to work in his field. The list goes on and on with people in the Bible who waited on the Lord for an event to happen or a dream to come to pass.

Waiting can seem like it is never-ending, like it lasts a lifetime, especially when time doesn't stand still and all your immediate friends move on with their lives. Your high school neighbor grows up, graduates from college, and is now engaged, and you are in your forties and still waiting for Mr. Fabulous.

Your friend's husband dies, and in the span of a year or two, she remarries. "What is wrong with me?" is often the cry of many singles. "Why do I have to wait so long? Has God forgotten me?" The cries and the questions go on, while God seems silent.

Carissa Meets Matthew

Carissa's wait for Mr. Fabulous was long and hard. Then she met Matthew at a Bible camp. He had a huge smile and played the drums with enthusiasm at chapel services. She was not attracted to him at first, but she was amused by his excitement.

He, in turn, was fascinated by her lively and dramatic personality as he watched her minister at evening chapel. His gaze was like an eagle's eye as he observed her in the chapel, in the dining room, and even on the playfield. She wondered to herself, *why is this man looking at me like this?*

Carissa and Matthew later discovered that they were in the same profession and shared many things in common. Carissa thought their first phone conversation would never end; in fact, she had to use her cell phone to dial her house number, pretending that another call was coming in, just to end the conversation. Talking to Matthew was easy, though. They were both Christians, they faced similar challenges on their jobs, and they were both health conscious.

The relationship blossomed over time. Matthew assisted Carissa with anything she needed. Carissa had just bought a house and Matthew was a handyman. He worked on the plumbing, fixed the heating system, helped her arrange the furniture, and even built permanent fixtures for the tenant quarters.

Matthew seemed to possess all the qualities of a perfect husband. To top it off, he was unusually respectful for a young single man who already had a child. Carissa was a virgin far past the age of thirty, but Matthew was already a father and had almost walked down the aisle with his son's mother. However, when he became a Christian, he decided to keep himself pure in order not to repeat his previous mistakes. Carissa thought his resolution admirable; she had no intention of being involved in a sexual relationship until marriage.

The two became inseparable. They hosted holiday dinners at her house. He met all her family and friends and they loved his easygoing personality. He visited her father during his long bout of illness and gave him his undivided attention. When Carissa's dad wanted somebody to talk to, he would call for Matthew. Carissa wondered if her dad was sharing his last wish, but later she found out that he was just showing his gratitude for Matthew's support and friendship.

Matthew and Carissa spent many Sunday evenings together, sometimes at her house and sometimes at his. At times, Matthew would take Carissa out to experience exquisite cuisines, and at other times, they would just walk in the park. As Carissa continued to pursue her studies, Matthew would edit her papers and encourage her to push forward. He was the perfect match, or so she thought.

One year of wonderful companionship quickly turned into two years. Still, Matthew was not ready to commit. Most girls after thirty, who are well into two years of a relationship, look forward to an impending engagement. Carissa was no different, but the years were slipping by and Matthew was in no form or shape ready to marry. He was not there yet. Carissa was frustrated. *Well, I am familiar with his likes and dislikes*, she thought. *I know his good and bad qualities, so I'll just wait. At some point, he will make a decision. Besides, I believe he loves me, and what guy loves a woman and invests so much time with her just to leave her?* Carissa consoled herself with these thoughts, but that was a big mistake.

Time passed and Carissa grew troubled and nervous. *Have I wasted all these years with this man, who still does not know if he is ready?* her heart spoke. Before she went to bed at night and on many lonely weekends, Carissa would cry out to the Lord, "Lord, help me! I can't take this anymore! What are You doing with me, Lord? What have I done? Lord, if my grandmother or my great-great-grandmother committed some terrible sin, forgive me, because I cannot understand why this is happening to me. Look at my friends. They start a relationship, and within a year or two they are married. Lord, what have I done wrong?" This went on for a long time.

One night, in the middle of a deep sleep, Carissa woke up to a still, small voice speaking in her heart: *Carissa, he is not the one.* Terrified, she thought, *Here I am, waiting and appealing to the Lord to change this man's heart from stone to flesh, and looking for a breakthrough, and this is what I'm hearing?* Trying to suppress the fear rising in her heart, she struggled to convince herself otherwise. *I wonder if the enemy is trying to trick me.*

For many days to come, the still, small voice continued to haunt her, but she blocked it out because it was not what she wanted to hear. She was in no shape to do without this guy. *Who will visit me and call me in those long winter months, in this country where nobody cares and where friends don't even answer their phones? Why should I give up the only person I have?* she reasoned within herself.

The decision to ignore the still, small voice would cost Carissa many years of regret, of fruitless waiting. As Christians, we know that God is a gentleman; He will not force Himself on anybody. He speaks and gives us a choice to obey or disobey. It is entirely up to us.

Carissa's friends were annoyed, hurt, and frustrated with her situation. They wanted the best for her and encouraged her to let the relationship go. One of her closest friends was so upset that she did not even want to hear Matthew's name or see him near Carissa. She totally isolated herself from the situation. Other friends encouraged Carissa to leave, telling her she did not deserve to wait on anybody for so long, and that she was worth more than that.

Carissa believed them, but could not seem to shake this guy. He was great company, he loved her, and he was there when her friends would not call or pick up the phone. *What do they expect me to do?* Carissa wondered to herself. *They are busy with their families, and I am here alone with nothing but the four walls for company. When I want somebody to talk to, they are not even available. They can talk all they want!* Carissa was stubborn.

A well-meaning friend encouraged her and Matthew to see a counselor. Matthew agreed that he needed this because he was suffering from anxiety at the thought of marriage. He was afraid that his marriage would fail like all the other marriages he knew of. To worsen the situation, he was afraid of emotional intimacy.

Carissa was hurt. *But then again, I can change him,* she thought. *If we go to a counselor, then Matthew will be able to see that this is just mind over matter. This is nothing for God to change,* she rationalized, forgetting that the Lord had already spoken specifically to her about the relationship. She continued to ignore that still, small voice that had said, *He is not the one.*

One of Carissa's pastors agreed to counsel with them. He was well-known and worked closely with the younger folks, and he was especially practical. The sessions started out well, and the counselor created a comfortable atmosphere for the young couple. He was extremely candid and supported both parties. As Matthew became more at ease, he began to let his hair down, sharing with the counselor things about Carissa that he wasn't comfortable with. He barely talked about himself, concentrating instead on Carissa and what she needed to change. This made her uncomfortable as she believed he was being evasive and not discussing the real issues.

After about twelve sessions, the counselor said, in his opinion, they were not ready to marry. Carissa was torn. How could this be? She couldn't wait any longer, and the counselor was adamant that she should move on. He believed Matthew had no intention to marry, and although he could not figure out what Matthew's demon was, he was sure Carissa needed to move on.

Embarrassed and ashamed, Carissa ended the relationship—or so she thought. Matthew was devastated. He couldn't sleep and began losing weight rapidly. One month turned into three, and before long, they were back together. "Give me six months, and I will get it together," he promised her. Convinced he would not repeat the same mistake, Carissa took him back. After six months, however, Matthew announced, "I am not there yet." How much could a girl suffer? This was too much to bear and she felt as if she were losing her mind.

At this point Carissa could not talk to her friends about her pain because they had given up on the situation and did not want to hear a word about Matthew. Her family members were equally done with the situation and thought she was wasting her time. Her mother was hurt to see her daughter in so much pain, but was helpless to do anything to help her. Carissa, and only Carissa, could make the choice to leave.

Once again, Carissa ended the relationship. The separation anxiety was again too much for them, and after another three months, they were back together. Matthew went to his pastor for counseling, and after much thought and prayer, he still felt he was not ready. Another pastor and counselor from Carissa's church counseled with Matthew, and yet again Matthew said he was not there yet. *What a cross to bear*, Carissa thought. *Why has this befallen me? So many invested years and still I am in this predicament. What is the Lord doing?* Again, she forgot the still, small voice that had said, *He is not the one.*

The relationship hit a brick wall. Matthew and Carissa were going around in circles. The pain of waiting was unbearable, but they continued with 'the evil' they knew. Matthew benefited from the companionship, while Carissa depended on the support; consequently, neither could set the other free. What a predicament.

Carissa spent countless hours on her knees, laboring about the situation. "Lord, help me. Help me, Father!" she cried. At times, she would pray, "Lord, change my heart in this situation. Align my will with Yours." On other occasions, she would pray, "Lord, what do You want from me? I have served You. I have remained faithful to You. What do You want from me, Lord?" Sometimes she would take another angle, "Lord, remove my shame. The younger women at church probably think I am worthless. How can I counsel them, when I cannot seem to get my act together?"

It was Christmastime and Carissa's anticipation of finally having a family of her own was growing stronger. She had told Matthew that she would not go into the New Year with an uncommitted relationship.

For the holidays, Carissa entertained as usual. She invited Matthew, as well as a family over for dinner. The evening was lovely. They sang, told stories of past Christmases, and shared gifts. After a beautiful evening, the family left, and Matthew went to the kitchen to do his usual cleanup. Carissa packed away the leftover food and cleaned the table, while Matthew washed the dishes and put away the pots and pans.

Now that they were alone, Carissa was anxious to open her gift. Matthew had placed it under the Christmas tree, which was perhaps a sign that it wasn't the gift she wished for. Nonetheless, she was hoping against hope. Matthew opened his gift first and was delighted with it. He received a huge box with about a hundred different types of tea. Since he loved to drink tea, Carissa had known he would be happy with the gift, and she was right.

Now it was her turn. The package was heavy, and she opened it with a sinking heart. It was a pair of sneakers. She was beside herself. *This man is brave!* she thought to herself and then expressed it aloud. "You are this brave?" she questioned him. Matthew sat holding onto his head, anticipating an explosion.

Carissa was calm, but the calmness soon turned into questions and the questions turned into tears. This time, however, the tears had new meaning. She knew this was the end of a remarkable friendship. Matthew did not speak as he watched Carissa cry. Heartbroken, she told him to leave.

The next day was devastating for Carissa. How could she have wasted so many years waiting on this one person? She could not sleep because she knew it was time to listen to the still, small voice, *He is not the one.*

The next two days were equally challenging. Matthew and Carissa talked on the phone. They had planned a previous engagement and decided to go through with it even though they had severed their ties. The evening was beautiful.

It was a sweet sixteen party, and Carissa and Matthew were inseparable. They went together and talked at dinner as if nothing had happened. She had never had such a lovely time with him. He was extremely attentive. It was as if they were a married couple. Nevertheless, she was determined not to go into the New Year with an uncommitted relationship.

Matthew seemed scared. This time Carissa made the unusual decision not to make a fuss. She was going to take a different approach to the situation, an approach that would bring closure and solid truth. "Matthew, you are a phenomenal person, and I just want to thank you for being there for me through thick and thin," she said. "Thank you for taking care of me when I needed a friend, and thank you for your love. I love you too and wish that it did not have to end this way, but I am asking you to set me free. I do not want to spend the rest of my life in a relationship that is not moving toward marriage, and I do not want to wait anymore."

Matthew listened intently. He reluctantly agreed.

Carissa continued speaking. "Matthew, I really wish you all the best in your future endeavors, but it is time to end this. I am not blaming you for anything, and I do not want you to blame yourself either. Our years of friendship were beautiful, and this is hard, but I have to go."

The two hugged and cried. They knew it was time.

What took Carissa so long to walk away? Was it the right time, or did she finally realize that she was wasting her time? *To everything, there is a season, and a time and purpose under the heaven,* says Ecclesiastes 3:1. Verse 8 goes on to say, *A time to love and a time to hate; a time of war, and a time of peace.* It was time for Carissa to move on. She had lingered, disobeyed, and tried to fix the situation. The time had come for her to let it go and let God.

CHAPTER 8

The Anxiety of Waiting

Some single girls experience much anxiety after seeing their close friends walk down the aisle one by one. They wonder, *What about me, Lord?* This unanswered question can rob a woman of her joy and leave her feeling isolated. The thought of not having her friends to share movie nights or a night out on the town can be daunting. This single state often seems like it is lasting a lifetime, especially when her girlfriends begin to have children and move on to other friends who share a similar life status. The isolation can overwhelm her; she does not fit in at the social gatherings for the married couples' group or in the group of younger people who are gearing up for college. What should she do?

Carissa was at that point of frustration after she broke up with Matthew. Her circle of friends was dwindling; most were busy with marriage and family, and others had moved to other states. Life wasn't the same. No longer was she the happy-go-lucky girl who could call a group of friends for girl's nights out, as they were no longer available. Her weekends were taken up with studies to pass the time, and although she was involved in church activities, it did not erase the pain of loneliness.

One day, Carissa was invited to a baby shower for her friend Toni. This was the norm for Carissa; she was a veteran in this sort of event. Baby showers, bridal parties, bridal showers, weddings—you name it. She was either a guest or an active participant in many.

This shower was different, though. The sun was bright, even though winter seemed to linger. Carissa's mood was on top of the world because she was going to celebrate the gift of a new life with Toni, one of her closest friends. Toni was the one who introduced her to new restaurants after she moved to New York, and Carissa had spent Christmas weekends with Toni's family. Although Toni had been married for over ten years, she still found time to overnight with Carissa for old time's sake.

Carissa was dressed and headed to the car with a huge bag of baby clothes and goodies for her friend. When she arrived, Toni's family was present in full number. Carissa was excited to see everyone and greeted them with hugs and kisses. Toni's two brothers were there with their wives and children. Another cousin was present with her two sons. Other mutual friends of Carissa and Toni began to show up with their kids, and even Toni's youngest nephew arrived with a toddler.

Like a flash of lightning, it occurred to Carissa that she was the only one there who wasn't married and who did not have a child. *Don't worry, girl. Don't think negatively. Your day will come.* Carissa secretly tried to console herself, but she could not shake the feeling of gloom. *Lord, what is wrong with me? Many of these people are not Christians, and they seem so happy with their families. I am older than many of them. What are You doing with me, Lord?* Carissa continued the private dialogue with Lord. Though she looked happy on the outside and was the life of the party, on the inside, her heart was crushed. *How could this happen to me? What have I done?*

Carissa left the baby shower that night with a broken heart. Her friends were oblivious to what was going on because she put on her best face. She took part in the games, shared jokes, cut the cake, and helped to clean up. By the look of things, Carissa was happy with life and doing great.

All that changed as soon as she reached the car door. The tears began to flow; she could hold them back no longer. Now that she was by herself, she could cry as loudly as she wanted. As she sat in the parking lot, tears rushed down her face like a waterfall. Carissa sobbed uncontrollably and spoke to her God. "Lord, I feel so embarrassed. I feel like a failure."

For the first time in her life, she was afraid to go home—afraid to face the empty house, afraid to meet the silence of the night.

Meet Payne and Her Husband, Greg

The next day Carissa received a call from one of her friends in Jamaica. Her former church was having their fiftieth anniversary celebration, and Payne, a childhood friend, wanted her to attend. They had been baptized the same year and shared dorms on camping trips.

Payne was extremely outgoing and could sing like a nightingale. Her group would always win the singing competition at the youth rallies, and she was popular with all the young men. During those years, it was their delight to take Payne on a date. Her tall physique, long dark hair, and beautiful copper complexion were the envy of most of the young ladies.

Carissa was grateful to have Payne as her friend. The girls complemented each other with their talents. Payne could sing and Carissa was the drama expert, so they ministered together during youth meetings and outreach programs in the community. When Carissa migrated to the United States, however, the girls lost contact, and Payne married her teenage sweetheart, Greg.

Greg wasn't Carissa's favorite person. Payne introduced him to her shortly after they were baptized, but Greg was often flirtatious. He even told Carissa that she would have been the one if he had not already met Payne, and that left a bad taste in her mouth. Greg could not be trusted.

To compound the situation, Greg was caught in a compromising position with Carissa's sister. When Payne found out, she was infuriated and refused to talk to him. Carissa was happy and encouraged her friend to be careful about the relationship. To her surprise, however, Greg found his way back into Payne's heart.

Carissa was troubled and prayed that Payne would do the right thing, but shortly after Carissa migrated to the United States, Payne and Greg were married. Carissa was disappointed, but Payne assured her that he was a changed man.

After years of separation, the two friends would finally meet again at the anniversary celebration. Carissa was excited. She was going home to her old familiar place, where the sounds of the falling mangoes brought gladness to her heart, just like the chirping of the birds in the wee hours of the morning.

She was beside herself with joy. "Yes, I am coming, Payne! Will you have a room where I can stay for the weekend?" she asked. There was a long pause on the phone. Carissa did not know what to think or what to do. Her friend should be happy to see her, and if she stayed with her, they would have more time to catch up on lost years.

"Um, let me get back to you on that, Carissa," replied Payne. "Let me speak to Greg first, and I will call you within the week," Payne assured her.

Hmmm, that is strange. It is the right thing to talk with your hubby before you make a decision, but why didn't she sound more excited? Carissa thought.

After a month, Carissa still had not heard from Payne, so she made other arrangements to stay with her sister Magda. The excitement over seeing Payne and her other friends distracted her from thinking about her breakup with Matthew. This vacation was timely and well-deserved.

The flight home felt strange. She hadn't been to Jamaica in years and did not know what to expect when she arrived. A few of her friends kept in touch with her through Facebook and WhatsApp, but it felt somewhat weird, though exciting, to actually have a chance to hug them and touch their faces.

The mixed feelings created a sense of anxiety, so much so that she left her laptop in the compartment section of the airplane and had to run back to the check-in area to reclaim it. That took a couple of hours, as the clerks sent her to several departments before she was finally able to retrieve it.

Magda was late in picking her up at the airport. After waiting for Carissa for a while, she decided Carissa must have missed her flight. She returned home, but when she got no call from her sister, she decided to check the airport again. Carissa was elated to see her, and the two talked all night, catching up on the lives of family members in both Jamaica and New York. Being home was great.

The next day was the anniversary service. Carissa was dressed before her sister. The excitement over seeing her childhood friends, her former pastors, and other church brothers and sisters gave her goose bumps. The anticipated jubilation was short-lived, however, when she got to the dining hall and saw Payne.

Payne was unrecognizable. She looked ten years older than what Carissa expected and appeared extremely fragile. *What has happened to my friend?* Carissa thought, beside herself with anguish. This was awkward because she did not know whether to run or cry. Instead, she forced a cheery greeting. "Hey, Payne! How are you?"

She gave her friend a tight hug and would not let go. Before she could speak again, Payne began to sob, and Carissa joined in. "My friend, my precious friend. You are finally here in the flesh," Payne managed to get out. And they hugged again.

The anniversary service was very rewarding for Carissa. Saints were awarded gold and silver plaques for their long years of service, and others paid tribute to leaders and believers who served the Lord faithfully in that ministry. Carissa was all smiles. As tributes were read, she reminisced about the good old days when she had grown up in that church.

She was delighted to see Danny and his wife. She was pleased to see the glow in their eyes as they looked at each other, but oh, how she wished for the day when she would have that same experience.

After the service, it dawned on Carissa that she had not seen Greg. She assumed he had stayed home with the kids, but then Payne brought the boys to greet her. "Payne, where is Greg?" she inquired.

"Oh, he doesn't attend church anymore. Besides, I don't know where he is at this time," Payne answered.

Carissa was surprised. Her friend had blurted out the information as if it were the norm. *Something is amiss*, she thought to herself. "Payne, can I see you for lunch tomorrow?" she asked.

"Well, I will get back to you in the morning and let you know for sure," replied Payne.

The next day Payne called early in the morning to say she could meet Carissa for lunch, but she could stay for only an hour. "That is wonderful," said Carissa. Although her weekend was packed with activities, and she had to leave on Monday morning to get home in time for work, she had to find out what was happening to her friend Payne, even if it meant canceling all her other appointments.

Payne and Carissa met at the dining room of the Pegasus Hotel. Carissa loved the friendly service and the charming ambiance. Exquisite paintings adorned every wall. The meal was pleasing to the eye with every color of the rainbow, and the fruit salad was carved in the shape of a ship.

Carissa was delighted to meet Payne. It had been a long time since the two had the chance to be alone together. The conversation began with light laughter as Payne filled in Carissa with the latest details of their friends and they reminisced about the past.

After half an hour of light conversation, Carissa shifted the topic. "How are you, Payne?"

"I am all right," the girl replied, her head looking down at the floor.

"Seriously, Payne, what is really going on with you? How is Greg? What is happening?"

Payne could not hold back the tears. "Carissa, I am so sorry I didn't listen to you when you told me to be careful about Greg. I haven't had a real marriage since the day I left for my honeymoon. Greg has been a real monster. He stopped going to church shortly after we were married, and he has not worked for years.

"We have moved from house to house because we could not afford the rent. I have been working at my grandmother's grocery store to put food on the table. Every work the man finds he leaves because he cannot get along with the boss. And, to make matters worse, he sleeps out some nights.

"I have tried to make the marriage work, but when I attempt to have a conversation with him about his behavior, he slaps me around in front of the kids.

"One Sunday morning, before I had to get the kids dressed for Sunday school, he walked in the house at 7:00 a.m. I was heading for the kitchen to prepare breakfast and decided not to say anything to him. But when I placed the food on the table, he sat down and looked at me like a bull ready to gobble up the food.

"I couldn't take it anymore, so I asked, 'Where are you coming from this hour of the morning, Greg?' Before I could utter another word, the man took the hot bowl of porridge and threw it in my face.

"Carissa, I am so unhappy with this person. He behaves like an animal sometimes. I was petrified to go to bed after the first night of the honeymoon. He was so impatient with me that I had to go to the doctor the following day."

Carissa was stunned. She sat in silence, just listening as her heart ached for her friend.

"Carissa, I don't believe in divorce. You know how we grew up in the church to understand that divorce is not an option, but I am tired of this. I feel that if I stay with him, I am going to lose my mind."

Carissa nodded and then spoke. "So, have you gone for counseling, Payne?"

"Well, I have gone to counseling, but Greg refuses to go. He has declined to speak to Pastor Jack, our new pastor. He claims that Pastor Jack cannot tell him anything because when he tried to talk to him, he took sides with me."

"Well, what are you going to do, Payne? You cannot continue to live like this. Besides, the children will be hurt when they witness the continual abuse."

Carissa was concerned. She could not tell her friend "I told you so," and she could not leave her without some form of support.

"Well, Payne, I am going to pray. And I want you to know that I am here for you. If you need any help with the kids or money for rent, I will send you help every month. But you must get out of this situation.

"I am not telling you to file for divorce, but if you are experiencing physical abuse, that is a serious matter. Not to mention, he is cheating and might well be exposing you to various forms of disease. Payne, the Lord values the sanctity of our lives; this could escalate into something more tragic, and someone might lose their life. You must find a way out of this situation for the sake of your kids, and for your own life."

Payne had to leave to pick up her son at school, and Carissa was late for her other appointment, so the girls said their good-byes.

Carissa was angry as she left the restaurant. *God, why?* she questioned the Lord as she sat in the cab. *You said Your purposes are past finding out, but I cannot understand the purpose of this. Payne was always so talented and had such a bright future. Then one mistake, one act of disobedience, caused her life to take such a drastic turn*, thought Carissa as she walked to her sister's apartment.

She arrived in New York shortly after twelve the following night. She could not get Payne out of her mind. The fright and the disappointment about her childhood friend's dilemma brought her to her knees night after night.

As she reasoned with the Lord, she thought about her own situation and the many times she had questioned the Lord. *I must repent*, she thought. *What disaster have You kept me from during all those years when You told me to wait? Lord, please forgive me for doubting You. I am sorry for being impatient when things didn't go my way. I am not rejoicing over Payne's misfortune, but what turn would her life have taken had she listened?*

After weeks of seeking the Lord, Carissa found peace. The Holy Spirit reassured her that He wasn't through with Payne and that His grace was sufficient to rescue her from this pitfall. She knew Payne was repentant and had acknowledged her mistake. Carissa also took comfort in the idea that the Lord's grace was enormous enough to cover her friend's sins and put her back on the path and purpose of her life.

What a wonderful and compassionate God we serve, she thought as she praised Him. *He knows we are frail and will make mistakes, but His mercies are new every morning. Great is His faithfulness* (see Lamentations 3:23).

Shortly after her visit to Jamaica, Carissa thought the pain of her breakup was waning. Her mind was so wrapped up in supporting Payne that she placed her own healing on the back burner. The reality of the breakup was about to resurface. This was the time in Carissa's life when her Savior would restore her joy in Him.

CHAPTER 9

When "No" Brings Joy

When God says no and you are left with a need, what do you do? Do you holler and bawl like a baby, or do you let go and fly like a bird? Waiting can leave questions lingering at the door of the heart of a single woman. She finds a great guy and enjoys spending time with him. They laugh and share the intimate details of life, but then he goes his merry way. Desire lingers like a fog hanging over a scorched field.

The counsel from friends and family feels especially cruel during this time. They say, "Maybe he was not the one. Just continue to trust God, and the right one will come along.

Enjoy your time with the Lord, and He will give you the desire of your heart."

This is a true statement, so the person who is suffering has no choice but to agree. However, when the rubber meets the road and friends begin to disappear, whom does she call in the middle of the night? She calls Jesus!

Mary and Martha had a different need. They wanted Jesus to come to them before their brother Lazarus died, but Jesus, calm as a cucumber, was in no hurry. The Scriptures recount that when Jesus heard that Lazarus was sick, He said, *"This sickness will not end in death. No, it is for God's glory so that God's Son may be glorified through it"* (see John 11:1–16).

Jesus seemed to take His own sweet time and waited two days before He started for Bethany. As He approached, He was met by the heartbroken sisters and the grieving crowd. Just to stretch your imagination a bit, imagine the sisters' greeting. "Jesus, where were You? If You had been here, our brother would still be alive. Now it is too late. If You had only come earlier, Lazarus would still be here." Imagine the lament.

The scene must have been extremely sad; in fact, it moved Jesus to tears (John 11:35). But "for His glory" was the word of the day. Jesus lingered so that the Son of Man would be glorified. That is the motivation of a loving, compassionate, and wise Father who calls His children to wait.

Mary and Martha must have been devastated to see their only brother take his last breath. They may have forgotten the healing power of their friend and Savior. Little did they know that after four days, the fetid, foul-smelling corpse would walk out from his grave, his clothing as pure as if he were an angel. Jesus—The Healer, the Way Maker—would show Mary, Martha and a multitude of other witnesses that He, the Son of Man, is the true and living God.

The wait must have felt like an eternity to Mary and Martha, but Jesus showed up just in time. Not only did He heal Lazarus, but He was also entrenched in their sorrow.

What a kind God He is. His purpose far exceeds our human understanding. He could have healed Lazarus before he died, but the miracle of raising him from the dead would speak loud and clear of His character as God, healer, and compassionate friend. And this Friend, Master, Deliverer, God, King, and Father works the same way in the lives of everyone He calls to wait.

Carissa Finds Healing

Carissa felt empty and alone after the breakup with Matthew. Sunday evenings were the hardest. She missed those countless hours they had spent watching a movie or dining out. She missed setting the table for her and Matthew to fellowship over a meal. She longed for the companionship in prayer they had shared as they committed their students to the Lord. She yearned for the lost laughter and moments of sharing and caring. Although their relationship had been void of physical contact, they had bonded over the years, knowing well each other's pet peeves and idiosyncrasies.

This was a hard pill to swallow. Her best friend could come no longer. She had to establish boundaries. She could no longer waste her precious time with someone who could not commit. That decision led her back to her first love, her Lord and Savior.

The song "I Miss My Time with You" by Larnelle Harris expressed it well and came as welcome comfort:

> There He was just waiting
> In our old familiar place

An empty spot beside Him
Where once I used to wait
To be filled with strength and wisdom
For battles of the day
I would have passed Him by again
But I clearly heard Him say
I miss My time with you
Those moments together
I need to be with you each day
And it hurts Me when you say
You're too busy, busy trying to serve Me
But how can you serve Me
When your spirit's empty
There's a longing in My heart
Wanting more than just a part of you
It's true
I miss My time with you

Carissa had to fall on her knees in repentance. You see, in all those years of waiting, she did not abandon either her fellowship at church or her ministry. Most importantly, she did not abandon her faith. However, during the years of focusing on her wait, she did lose contact with the Savior.

Now she had to thrust herself into His arms to survive the heartbreak. She had to drown her thoughts in His Word in order to find strength for each day. And, in talking with Him, she found a new way to love Him. Those moments together with Him took her back to when she was fifteen, when she first met Him and could not stop singing. She felt a fresh sense of intimacy with her Lord and it was good.

She had been barren and dejected, but now she could draw water from the well that was springing up within her. Carissa could not depend on friends and family to lift her out of the pit of despair; she had to fix her eyes on her king, her friend, her Lord, and her closest companion, if she was going to survive the breakup.

Carissa made a simple and profound decision to turn off her television. This was a sacrifice, as tuning in to the news was the first thing she did after arriving home from her job each day. She was a news junkie indeed and often debated with her friends about the latest political events on CNN. She would scold her mother and coworkers about their lack of knowledge regarding current events. "You should be aware of what is happening around the world. How can you live like that?" Carissa would say.

Giving up television was also a big sacrifice because it meant she could no longer watch her *Lifetime* movies, *Blue Bloods*, and *Hawaii Five-O*. Judge Judy and Dr. Phil were another part of her evening ritual, and she missed watching them.

This decision was necessary to help Carissa make it through the days of emptiness and barrenness. She had to spend some quality time with her Savior because she needed peace, and she needed it desperately. After the breakup, she experienced a deep urgency for something more, something new, something that would prevent her from going over the deep end.

It is amazing how disappointment and heartbreak often prompt a person to the foot of the cross. Meesha, Carissa's childhood friend, had given her a journal for Christmas. Little did they know that the Lord would take Carissa on a journey of solitude a couple of weeks later and that she would need to start journaling about her spiritual road trip.

Each evening Carissa raced home from work to meet with the Lord. She was engaged in a study called "Detour," which was based on the book of Genesis, with emphasis on the story of Joseph. Carissa was so wrapped up in the Bible that she could not put it down. The story of Joseph came at a pivotal time in her life; she easily related to the twists and turns his life took in order for him to reach his destiny. She took notes, cried, and wrote her prayers from the Word.

Weeks turned into months. The pain of the breakup began to subside. Her newfound purpose was luring her like a shark to blood to immerse herself in the Word. After a few months, she was rushing to get home; she could not find time to talk with her friends on the phone because her focus was shifting. Jesus, her friend and lover, was becoming her first love all over again.

As weeks progressed, Carissa's prayer time grew longer. She was checking off answered prayers about the friends and family members she had committed to the Lord, and she had peace that was far past her understanding. This was the girl who should have been mourning the loss of a long-term relationship, but instead, she was tapping into the well of living water deep within her. That living water from the Holy Spirit enveloped her entire spirit. She felt joy, as if it were the first day of spring after a hard winter, and she did not want it to end. It was like falling in love with Him all over again.

Months went by and she found herself getting up at three and four in the quiet hours of the morning just to talk with her Lord and lover. It was as if she could not get enough of Him and did not want to let Him go. At times, she felt tired, but the Holy Spirit would give her a nudge, and she would get up. It was as if someone were touching her and breathing over her.

The sound of the birds was absent on those mornings. The tooting of the horns from cars and school buses were not heard as Carissa spoke with her Abba Father. As He ministered to her through His Word, she learned a new way of listening to His voice. The relationship became so intimate that Carissa would speak to Him as if she were talking to a friend sitting close to her.

With each month, her interest in television and talking with friends on the phone faded even more. Her pain took her into a new sphere of devotion to her heavenly Father. Her worship time imparted new strength and hope; she did not want to let go of the hem of His garment. Her friends began to ask, "Why are you looking so radiant, Carissa? Have you found a new guy? What is new with you?" Carissa would only smile because she alone knew her secret.

Of course, there were days when she would regress and miss Matthew terribly, but she wasn't afraid to cry. The tears brought the healing she needed. The pain and feeling of abandonment eventually gave her a new outlook on life. She wasn't going to settle for anything less than the best. Matthew was gone and she wasn't going to allow him to step back through her door without a commitment. She refused to sell herself short anymore. Her Savior was enough. He was the fulfillment she needed. Little by little, in every day and in every way, Jesus was changing her.

Oftentimes we think that transformation happens once and for all at the time of our conversion, but with each experience we have in life, God is breaking, molding, and making us into special and selected vessels of honor. The wait may be longer than we expect. At times, we may think the wait is over, only to have Him take us on another journey of wait. What do we do? Crumble?

Job's wife told him to curse God and die when he lost everything, but Job would not yield. He praised the Lord even more. Later his test became his testimony and his pain resulted in gain. At the end of his journey, he received a double portion of his wealth and the children he had previously lost (See Job).

Carissa had waited for Mr. Fabulous all her life. This next point might seem trivial to many devoted Christian folks, but God said it is not good for a man to be alone. That goes for a woman as well. The church often prays over a man and helps him seek a wife when the years are passing by and he is still single. The same is not true for a woman who is far past thirty and even approaching fifty. She is often told that God did not intend for everyone to be married. With that, many well-intentioned single women find themselves looking for a man outside their Christian circle. Others, however, continue to wait their turn. *If I have waited this long, I may as well continue*, they think.

The determination of some faithful singles eventually leads them to find Mr. Fabulous in their forties or even fifties but then, the question of having children bombards them. Trying to avoid that scenario, some misguided singles leave the church, have their babies, and then return like the Prodigal Son. This path is full of much trepidation and sorrow, and they wonder if it was worth it.

Carissa was willing to wait, even though her experience was difficult. She witnessed far too many friends walking down the aisle to their dream mates, leaving her behind to catch the bouquet. But it was all to avail—no man. A time came when she refused to dance to Beyoncé's song "I Am a Single Lady" while waiting in line to catch the bouquet. She had had enough. She had also had enough of being a bridesmaid or a maid of honor. Her first wedding as a maid of honor was delightful because she was only seventeen, but now she was into her eighth and ninth weddings as a bridesmaid, and it was enough. *No more*, she told herself.

This last breakup, the one with Matthew, was it too. Her Lord and lover would be her only desire now, and she wasn't going to allow herself to get into another hurtful relationship. She was done giving her time and attention to a man and receiving nothing but an air balloon in return. No more—and that was final.

As Carissa continued to spend time with her Lord, a sense of true fulfillment developed. She missed Matthew a little less, and on the occasions that he did call, she was busy. She also frequented the Christian bookstore and began reading a wide variety of Christian genres. She found herself ignoring phone calls, as she was now more interested in feeding her inner soul and mind.

Carissa was growing deep within. As the deer pants for the water brook, so was her soul thirsting after her Savior (see Psalm 42:1). As the months passed, she slowly became whole. No longer did she long for company to fill her time. She no longer dreaded going home alone on weekdays or returning from church on Sundays. She wasn't afraid to sit at a restaurant alone and enjoy a sumptuous meal.

Carissa was enjoying her own company. The woman that God was molding all along through her ups and down, through her pain and strain, was now learning to like herself. She was learning to cook a nice meal for herself, to set the table with the best china and silverware and then enjoy it alone.

Carissa's newfound desire to spend more time with her Lord taught her that waiting wasn't so bad after all. The actual meaning of the verse *Delight thyself in the Lord, and he shall give you the desires of your heart* (Psalm 37:4 KJV) was becoming real. The delighting—that was the part that had been missing all along. But now Carissa was learning that when she delighted in Him during the wait, she was not focusing on the "what" she was waiting for, but rather on the One she was waiting for. That reality became the essence of her joy.

Mary and Martha waited a few days for Jesus to come to Bethany; however, He did not show up until Lazarus was already dead. Why did He take so long? If He had been there earlier, the pain and the sorrow could have been avoided. But God—He had a plan! He showed His true character before, during, and after the wait.

In her pain, Carissa found Jesus as if it were the first time. Through her sorrow, she fell in love with her Master, Maker, and Savior all over again. And she was still waiting.

Chapter 10

Wait for What?

Sometimes we hear of a person who misses a flight and later discovers their life was mysteriously saved when the plane suffered an engine failure and crashed, leaving no surviving passengers. Such news often jerks us back to the reality that our lives are controlled by a supreme being. Our busy schedules become less pressing, and we begin to think of the people who are most important to us.

A single woman sometimes feels betrayed by the Lord when she has to give up a long-standing relationship and later learns that her fiancé found someone new and married only a year after they broke up. That is not easy. This kind of news has the propensity to spiral a girl's emotions into the sea of depression to the point where she needs a lifeguard to pull her out.

"What is God doing? What does He want from me?" is often the cry of many girls who have waited the best part of their lives to find Mr. Fabulous. They follow the rules, believe, and wait, while time seems to fly away from them.

Abraham and Sarah waited twenty-five years for their promised child, Isaac. The wait was long and difficult and progressed to the point where Sarah became impatient with God and decided to help Him out. The woman must have complained to God a million times. Imagine the sobbing and the angry outbursts poor Abraham had to endure. "Abraham, I don't know, but maybe God has forgotten us. Perhaps you misinterpreted what He meant by thinking He intended to give you a son from my womb."

I can just imagine how frustrated Abraham must have felt to give in to her demands by lying with her maid in order to produce a child. Think of the sorrow in his heart when years later He had to face the consequence of His mistake and give notice to the maid and her son to leave his home because of the same wife who had encouraged him to help God out.

But God! Though Abraham and Sarah sinned against the Lord, His mercy was more than enough to cover their sins. The promised Isaac was born after twenty-five years of waiting. You see, my friends, it doesn't matter to God what we have done (though we still face the consequences of our disobedience). He still takes us to the predetermined location He planned for us.

When God designs a plan for our lives, it is not dependent on our perfection or imperfection. No, the Lord knew ahead of time that we would falter and fail. The most remarkable part of this journey is that He knows how to get us back on the right path despite the shifts and turns in our lives. He knows the detours, shortcuts, and bypasses and has already calculated the entire route for our lives.

The story of Carissa is simple compared to many. However, her search for a mate landed her in many unexpected places and eventually led her right back to her Savior, her first love. If we evaluate her life, we might think she was unfortunate to have her parents leave her at a tender age, but when Jesus took her up as His own child, she got the chance to know Him in a unique and personal way. He became her source of comfort in her disappointments and heartaches. He became her true companion during the lonely and stressful years of her singleness. He was her strength when nobody else was there to call on. Carissa's relationship with her Lord was unique to her, and He had a special purpose that was designed for her alone.

Carissa's story is not yet finished. She may or may not find her Mr. Fabulous, but one thing is sure: her Savior has a providential plan for her in the twists and turns of her life in order to take her to her destiny.

Why Wait?

So, my answer to the question, *wait for what?* will probably disappoint some. On the other hand, perhaps it will encourage many singles and even married folks who have waited many years for their dreams to be realized.

Hebrews 11 recounts the many saints who waited patiently on the Lord and shows us that God will perform all He has promised to us in Christ. These stars of faith give us examples to live by. Their lives were by no means laid out on a platter for them; rather, they made the Hall of Faith through the various testings and trials they endured. Some were put to death, others sawed in two, and still others killed by the sword. They went about in the skins of sheep and goats—destitute, persecuted, and mistreated (see verse 37).

These heroes of faith lived true to the saying "no pain, no gain." Enoch was commended for pleasing God (verse 5). Noah was warned about the flood, and he and his family were saved (verse 7). Abraham and Sarah received their promise (verse 17), and as the commendations continue, many more saints walked in their destinies through faith. The faith of these saints is a classic example of how we should live as Christians, whether we are married or single.

You see, my friends, there is not one specific answer to the question of why we should wait. Rather, every individual needs to walk with God, like Abraham and Enoch did, in order to discover the specific plan and purpose He has designed for them. Sometimes He does not immediately reveal His plans to us, but as we walk closer to Him, He unfolds His purposes step by step. This walk requires simple faith, since we do not know why and how He will lead us. If we continue to trust Him, we will surely walk the path He has specially orchestrated for us.

The faithful and righteous patriarchs, Enoch and Abraham, walked with God, but their paths were different. Enoch did not see death on this earth, while Abraham lived 175 years and then died. God had a different journey for the two men and His purposes were fulfilled individually in their lives. Abraham became the father of a sea of people, and Enoch's life serves as an example that a person can live so righteously that he does not see death.

So why should we wait? The simplest answer, I think, is for God's purposes to be realized in our lives. As we wait and walk, we will learn more about our Savior. We will learn to live righteously, and we will grow. Our trust in Him will become solid.

Waiting Tests Our Commitments

Waiting can grow into our best friend when we realize it affords us the opportunity to discover our true reason for waiting. People who desire a blessing right away are not interested in commitment. A single man who gets upset when a girl tells him to wait and who then runs off to marry the next available woman (sometimes on rebound) will buckle under pressure when problems appear in the marriage. Yes, problems will occur, and the person who struggles with commitment will be the first to quit on a marriage.

For example, I heard of a woman who decided she did not want to be married anymore once she learned that her spouse had diabetes. She felt it was too much to care for a man who might not function in the matrimonial bed as before, so she left him to find another man who would satisfy her more.

Another story is told of a girl who went to marriage counseling because she could not understand why it was so difficult for her husband to lift the toilet seat when he urinated. She could not get over his sloppiness and was ready to bolt. To her surprise, she learned in the counseling session that he was annoyed that she did not know how to make a bed neatly or cook his favorite stew peas soup. What distinguished the two was that the husband was committed to working it out, but the wife was ready to flee because of her pet peeves.

So, my friends, sometimes the Lord in His wisdom allows us to wait in order to mature us into committed adults—and commitment is the main ingredient for a successful marriage. Commitment is necessary to develop stamina when trials and tribulation shake our world, as they surely will. When we feel like running away from home because we do not have enough money to pay all the bills, commitment is pivotal.

Waiting Builds Patience

Patience is a virtue and an essential ingredient for marriage. An impatient Christian girl becomes frustrated in marriage when the baby needs changing and she has to stay awake at night to put that child back to sleep.

It takes patience to live through disagreements, especially when the man wants to save up more money to buy a house and the woman wants to move right away. It takes patience when an in-law takes over the spare room and seems to have no plans of leaving, and the spouse takes forever to give notice to the relative.

Patience is necessary when the man experiences a midlife crisis and begins to salivate after the younger sisters in the church. That wife has to stay on her knees for him until the storm passes. It takes patience to wait for a husband to come home and cut the grass and paint the kitchen, while he is at church fixing the roof and driving every senior citizen home after church.

Love is kind and patient, and that is the word of the hour. The story is told of a man who had enough of his marriage and felt that since the children were gone, it was time for him to seek a fresh start. He announced to his wife that he had found somebody else and was leaving by the end of the month. The wise and patient woman did not shed a tear. She was as calm as a cat, asking only that her husband lift her out of bed every morning and take her to the dining table before he left for work. Out of guilt, he agreed to the strange request.

The first days were a bit difficult, and he wondered what the point was. On the fifth day, however, as he carried his wife, the smell of her perfume reminded him of the first day they met. The tenth day, as he lifted the woman from the bed, he noticed that she looked happier than she had in years. Then, on the twenty-fifth day, he noticed that he was enjoying the fact that he was making his wife happy. This time he did not want to put her down. By the thirtieth day, they were kissing the way they had in the early days of their marriage. On the final day of the month, he announced that he wanted to renew their vows.

Patience can produce solid results. The woman did not plan on her husband's reaction, but her patience produced more than she could ever have imagined. His response to her request to lift her out of bed each day unearthed the buried love they still shared. The two were at a new place.

My friends, sometimes God makes us wait in order to teach us patience to handle future trials. If we do not possess this virtue, we will surely walk away from a good marriage when a little trouble comes, or we will leave a job when the boss is unreasonable or a coworker gets our well-deserved promotion.

Waiting Transforms Our Character

Similar to unbelievers, many of us Christians have baggage in our lives. It is only the saving grace of Jesus that covers and renders us different from the world. When people rub us the wrong way, they would likely be surprised if they could know what we are thinking. Sometimes a fly on the wall knows our character much better than our closest friends, because we do certain things only when we think no one else is looking.

Our wise heavenly Father sometimes allows us to wait so that He can break, mold, and shape us into vessels that will be ready to live with others and share our lives with them. Romans 12:1 talks about the need for believers not to be conformed to this world, but to be transformed by the renewing of their minds, so that they may prove the good, acceptable, and perfect will of God.

The trial of waiting is a perfect way for transformation to take place because suffering often pulls us closer to God, as it did in the case of Carissa. After she experienced so much heartache, she started to dig deeper into the Word. The more time she stayed on her knees, the more she wanted to because the Lord was changing her desire for things that would harm her and helping her develop a total trust in Him. She was enjoying Him more and more. Although the emptiness and the longing for companionship were still evident, she was satisfied spending time by herself.

Nothing is wrong with falling in and out of love, but when the focus is on the need instead of on the Lord, we miss the opportunity to be content and fulfilled in Him. When we learn how to do this, our worldview about love and relationships is no longer influenced by Hollywood, but by God, the one who knows what our future looks like. Our trust in Him is deepened with our total surrender.

Spending quality time in prayer and the Word creates in us a sense of wholeness. No longer are we in a frenzy to find others to go out with. Rather, we spend our time on purposeful living as we look to Him for guidance in every decision we make. We are proving what is good for us when we live in obedience to His Word and patiently wait for His perfect will to be realized in our lives. This conforming to his Word helps us to be transformed, so that we can prove what is His good and perfect will for us, whether we are single or married.

Waiting Builds Intimacy

What is intimacy? It is sharing our innermost secrets and thoughts with someone. It is talking with them throughout the day, and it is spending most of our time with them. A single woman, as well as the married woman, has the opportunity to develop that kind of relationship with the Lord.

The apostle Paul stated in 1 Corinthians 7:7 that he wished all were single as he was, but he also acknowledged that everyone has a unique gift from God. I believe that most singles, who wait on God, will eventually find a partner, but I also believe that some will commit to a life of singleness based on the specific call that God has for them. As singles, it is paramount that our intimacy with Him be nurtured because that is how we will know what He has called us to do. We need to definitely know whether we should wait or go ahead and marry. You see, my friends, intimacy with God is critical as we wait for Him to work in our lives.

Waiting often causes us to stay on our knees, and if we are there too long and nothing happens, we tend to give up. Hannah waited a long time to have a child. I can imagine how she must have lamented when her husband's other wife provoked and ridiculed her for being unable to bear a child. The embarrassment must have been overwhelming, but Hannah had a secret: her prayer life.

The intimacy Hannah shared with her Lord must have inspired her to give her son back to Him after God answered her prayer. I am fascinated by this story because Hannah's heart was in the right place. She wanted a son, and she went to the temple all by herself to beseech the throne of God. She refused to give up, and in fact, her intercession was so fervent that the priest thought she was drunk. When she explained to the priest what she wanted from the Lord, he blessed her and agreed with her in prayer.

My favorite part of the story follows, as Hannah immediately began praising God. She knew that her prayer was answered even before she went home to her husband. Her song of gratitude is an example of the true worship that intimacy brings (see 1 Samuel 1). The point is God is interested in the journey of waiting for reasons beyond the thing we are waiting for. On the journey, He reveals to us the intimate details of His plans.

You see, my friends, waiting has a way of inducing a type of intimacy that God wants from us. When we wait for Him, it takes us to a different level of prayer. We listen to Him keenly, we talk to Him about everything, and we enjoy His comfort and peace in the midst of waiting. We learn more about Him as we dwell in His secret place (see Psalm 91).

So, my friends, though the wait seems long, we must trust, we must pray, we must praise—and we must wait. As we wait, without complaint and groans, let's look at a poem that reflects the proper attitude of our hearts.

Wait for What?
Though the fig tree does not bud, and there are no grapes on the vine,
And there is no Mr. Fabulous to call mine,
Still, I wait.
Though the years turn into decades,
And there are no more comrades,
Still, I wait.
Though there are no babies in the crib,
And my neighbors laugh and glib,
Still, I wait.
Though my bed is empty and my arms are bare,
And in the ceiling alone at nights I stare,
Still, I wait.
Still, I wait! For the Master knows my name.
I will be still and know that for me, He has a noble aim.

Discussion Questions for Small-Group Study

I hope the following questions will stir lively debates in youth fellowships,

* Do you think the church is equipped to tackle the challenges faced by single women in the twenty-first century? Explain your answer.

* How long should a girl wait in a relationship before expecting a proposal? Should she even have this expectation in the first place? Discuss.

* If a man says he is not ready for a commitment after a year in a serious relationship, should the woman bolt? What are your reasons for your answer?

* Do you think it is permissible for a man and a woman to have a platonic relationship in which they spend time together praying, shopping, dining out, and going to the movies? Discuss your viewpoint.

* Do you think it is right for a man to spend quality time visiting a woman at her home and taking her places if he has no intention of engaging her in a committed relationship?

* Carissa faced many difficulties growing up, including parental neglect. Do think this contributed to the struggles she faced in dating? Why or why not?

* Carissa broke up with Christopher, her first boyfriend, after experiencing restless nights and haunting dreams about their engagement. Do you think this was a good-enough reason to break up? Why or why not?

* Do you think the Lord can speak to His children about a relationship in the form of a dream? What are some Bible verses that support your view?

* Carissa's mother and father neglected her at a young age. If you had been in her situation, what would you have done after your parents came back into your life?

* Carissa's childhood friend Payne found herself in a difficult marriage after marrying a man who she knew was "bad news." What advice would you give a friend if you discovered she was in an abusive marriage?

* On what grounds, if any, should a Christian consider divorce? Provide Scripture references to support your response.

* Carissa forgave her father for neglecting her at a young age; however, do you think it was

important for him to apologize to her after those many years? Why or why not?

* As a young Christian woman, what would you do if you waited on the Lord for a life partner until you were forty, but still had found no one?

* What would you do if, as a married woman, you realized you had made a mistake and married the wrong man? What would you do if you reached the point in your marriage where you were afraid to go home after work?

* What encouragement would you give a married woman who has fallen out of love with her spouse because of the way he treats her?

* What encouragement would you give to a single woman who has waited all her life for a life partner, and she is now approaching the end of her childbearing years?

* Do you think a single Christian woman should adopt a child, or should she wait to have a child after she has married? Explain your reasoning.

* Do you think a Christian woman should entertain the idea of in vitro fertilization? Give Scripture verses to support your thoughts.

* Do you think it is permissible for a Christian married couple to consider surrogacy after failing to conceive for years? Support your answer with Scripture references.

* How should a young single woman respond to a person who keeps prodding her about why she is not married?

* How should a woman, who has been unable to conceive after years of marriage, respond to the constant nudging from others who want to know why she has not had a baby?

Printed in the USA
CPSIA information can be obtained
at www.ICGtesting.com
LVHW092008300124
770322LV00004B/124